BEYOND THE DRESS

BEYOND THE DRESS

A Comprehensive Guide to Inclusive Wedding Planning for Gay Men

TYLER DOZER

Illuminated Ideas Publishing

CONTENTS

CHAPTER 1

Introduction

Welcome to "Beyond the Dress: A Comprehensive Guide to Inclusive Wedding Planning for Gay Men." We're thrilled to embark on this exciting journey with you as we delve into the multifaceted world of planning a wedding that authentically reflects your love story. In these pages, we'll navigate the joyous path toward your special day, ensuring that every element of your celebration resonates with the uniqueness of your relationship.

The landscape of weddings has evolved, and so too have the narratives surrounding them. No longer bound by tradition or constrained by societal norms, today's weddings are a canvas for individuality, diversity, and love in all its splendid forms. In this book, we celebrate the beauty of same-sex unions, recognizing the distinctive aspects that make gay weddings a tapestry of love, acceptance, and personal expression.

As we begin this exploration, we invite you to take a moment to reflect on your vision as a couple. What makes your love extraordinary? How can your wedding day encapsulate the essence of your relationship? From the grand gestures to the subtle nuances, we're here to guide you through the process of translating your unique connection into a memorable celebration.

Throughout "Beyond the Dress," inclusivity takes center stage. We acknowledge the rich tapestry of the LGBTQ+ community, with a particular focus on the experiences of gay men. This book is a comprehensive resource designed to empower you, offering insights, advice, and inspiration to navigate the intricacies of wedding planning. Whether you're just starting or fine-tuning the details, we're here to be your companions on this exhilarating journey.

In the chapters ahead, we'll explore everything from envisioning your dream ceremony to selecting the perfect venue, crafting personalized vows, and addressing the specific needs of trans men in wedding planning. So, let's dive in, celebrate love in all its forms, and create a wedding day that goes "Beyond the Dress," telling a story that is uniquely and unequivocally yours.

Understanding the Modern Landscape of Gay Weddings

Understanding the Modern Landscape of Gay Weddings

In recent years, the landscape of weddings has undergone a remarkable transformation, reflecting the evolving attitudes and acceptance of diverse expressions of love. As we embark on this journey of wedding planning for gay men, it's essential to recognize and appreciate the significant strides made in the realm of same-sex unions.

Historically, societal norms and legal restrictions constrained the possibilities for LGBTQ+ couples. However, as we stand on the precipice of a new era, the narrative surrounding weddings has shifted dramatically. The concept of a traditional wedding has broadened to encompass a spectrum of celebrations, each uniquely tailored to the individuals committing to a life together.

One of the most remarkable aspects of the modern landscape of gay weddings is the celebration of authenticity. Couples are no longer confined to predetermined roles or expectations; instead, they are empowered to create ceremonies that authentically reflect their personalities, beliefs, and love stories. This shift has given rise to a diverse tapestry of weddings, each telling a unique tale of love and commitment.

Moreover, the legal landscape has witnessed substantial progress. With increasing recognition of LGBTQ+ rights, many countries and regions have embraced marriage equality. This not only signifies a triumph for civil rights but also opens up a world of possibilities for couples who can now legally wed and celebrate their love in a way that was once denied to them.

In this context, the concept of marriage has transcended its traditional boundaries. Gay weddings are no longer seen as a deviation from the norm but rather as a celebration of love in all its forms. This shift has contributed to a more inclusive and accepting society, where diverse expressions of love are not only acknowledged but celebrated.

Technology and social media have played a pivotal role in reshaping the narrative of gay weddings. Couples now have platforms to share their stories, providing inspiration and support to others in the community. The visibility of diverse love stories has helped break down stereotypes and foster a sense of community, creating a virtual space where couples can connect, share advice, and celebrate their unique journeys.

As we navigate the modern landscape of gay weddings, it's important to recognize the pioneers who paved the way for the acceptance and celebration of LGBTQ+ love. Their courage and resilience have contributed to the changing attitudes that allow couples today to plan weddings that reflect their true selves.

In the chapters that follow, we will delve into the various aspects of wedding planning for gay men, exploring how you can infuse your ceremony with authenticity, navigate the legalities, and embrace the diverse traditions that make your union special. So, let's continue this journey with an open heart and a deep appreciation for the modern landscape that allows us to celebrate love in all its beautiful forms.

Navigating Legalities and Celebrating Equality

In the realm of wedding planning for gay men, it's crucial to recognize the legal landscape that shapes the journey toward marriage. While love knows no boundaries, legalities can sometimes present challenges that require careful consideration and navigation.

The significant strides made in LGBTQ+ rights have paved the way for marriage equality in many parts of the world. However, it's important to be aware of the specific legal requirements and regulations that may vary depending on your location. Begin your wedding planning journey by understanding the legalities surrounding same-sex marriages in your region.

First and foremost, check the legal status of same-sex marriages in your country or state. Laws can vary, and staying informed about the latest updates is essential. Fortunately, the trend toward marriage equality has been gaining momentum, but it's always wise to confirm the current legal standing to ensure a smooth and stress-free planning process.

Once you've established the legal parameters, familiarize yourself with the required documentation for obtaining a marriage license. This may include identification, proof of residency, and any additional documents stipulated by local authorities. Ensuring you have all the necessary paperwork in order well in advance will prevent last-minute hiccups and allow you to focus on the joyous aspects of your celebration.

In some cases, you may encounter challenges related to religious or cultural beliefs that may impact the legal recognition of your marriage. It's essential to approach these situations with openness and patience, seeking guidance from LGBTQ+ organizations, legal experts, or religious leaders who can provide insights and support.

Celebrating equality goes beyond legal recognition—it extends to the heart of your wedding ceremony. Embrace the opportunity to craft a celebration that reflects not only your love for each other but also your commitment to equality and inclusivity. This could mean incorporating symbolic elements into your ceremony that highlight the journey toward equality or choosing vendors who actively support and celebrate LGBTQ+ unions.

As you navigate the legalities, remember that you are part of a broader movement that has advocated for and achieved significant milestones in LGBTQ+ rights. Take pride in the progress made, and let it inspire you as you plan a wedding that not only celebrates your love but also contributes to the ongoing narrative of equality.

Consider reaching out to LGBTQ+ advocacy groups or legal professionals specializing in LGBTQ+ rights for additional support and resources. Their expertise can be invaluable in navigating any legal complexities that may arise during your wedding planning journey.

In the chapters ahead, we'll delve deeper into the practical aspects of legal considerations, providing guidance on obtaining marriage licenses, addressing potential challenges, and ensuring that your wedding day is a celebration of love and equality. So, let's continue this journey with confidence, armed with the knowledge that love is a force that can overcome any legal hurdle, and your celebration is a testament to the progress we've collectively achieved.

Embracing Diversity in Wedding Traditions

In the kaleidoscope of wedding planning for gay men, one of the most exciting and meaningful aspects is the opportunity to embrace and celebrate the rich tapestry of diverse wedding traditions. Your love story is unique, and your wedding should be a reflection of that individuality, drawing inspiration from various cultural, religious, and personal traditions that resonate with you as a couple.

As we embark on this exploration of diverse wedding traditions, it's essential to recognize that love knows no boundaries. Your wedding ceremony can be a beautiful fusion of traditions that honor your backgrounds, beliefs, and the journey that led you to this moment.

Consider starting by reflecting on your individual cultural and religious backgrounds. Whether you come from the same cultural heritage or diverse backgrounds, this is an opportunity to explore the rituals and customs that hold significance for both of you. It might involve incorporating traditional attire, rituals, or symbols that pay homage to your respective backgrounds, creating a unique blend that tells the story of your unity.

Moreover, feel empowered to create new traditions that speak specifically to your relationship. Traditions are not only about honoring the past but also about forging a path for the future. This could be as simple as establishing a special ceremony or ritual that holds personal significance for you both, whether it's exchanging heartfelt letters before the ceremony or planting a tree together as a symbol of growth and endurance.

Consider involving your families in the process, opening up conversations about the traditions that hold sentimental value for them. This collaborative approach not only deepens the emotional connection to your wedding but also fosters understanding and unity among your families.

Inclusivity is a key theme in embracing diverse wedding traditions. As gay men, your wedding has the power to challenge stereotypes and break down barriers. Be intentional in your choices, ensuring that the traditions you incorporate are inclusive and welcoming to all your guests, regardless of their backgrounds or beliefs.

Remember that your celebration is an opportunity to showcase the beauty of love in all its forms. Whether you draw inspiration from cultural, religious, or personal traditions, let your wedding be a testament to the diverse and inclusive love that exists within the LGBTQ+ community.

Throughout the upcoming chapters, we'll explore specific traditions, rituals, and ceremonies that you may consider incorporating into your wedding. From blending cultural elements to crafting personalized vows, each choice you make contributes to the rich tapestry of your wedding day. So, let's continue this journey of embracing diversity with open hearts, celebrating the uniqueness of your love story, and creating a wedding that reflects the beauty of unity in all its forms.

CHAPTER 2: GETTING STARTED

Welcome to Chapter 2: Getting Started, a pivotal phase in your wedding planning journey. Now that you've embarked on this exciting adventure of celebrating love in all its forms, it's time to lay the foundation for the wedding of your dreams. This chapter is your compass, guiding you through the initial steps that will set the tone for the entire planning process.

Getting started is not just about ticking off a to-do list; it's about defining your vision as a couple and translating that vision into a roadmap for your wedding day. Your love story is unique, and your wedding should be an authentic reflection of the bond you share. In these pages, we'll explore the essential elements that will shape your celebration, from envisioning the overall vibe to practical considerations like budgeting and timelines.

Let's start by delving into the heart of your vision. What does your dream wedding look like? Is it an intimate gathering in a rustic setting, a vibrant city celebration, or perhaps a destination wedding that reflects your adventurous spirit? Your vision is the North Star that will guide you through the myriad of decisions you'll make along the way.

Budgeting wisely is the next crucial step. It's not just about numbers; it's about aligning your financial plan with your wedding vision. We'll explore practical tips and strategies to help you allocate resources efficiently, ensuring that every dollar contributes to creating the magical experience you desire.

Setting a realistic timeline is equally vital. Whether you're planning a grand celebration or an intimate affair, time is your ally. From booking the perfect venue to selecting vendors and finalizing details, a well-thought-out timeline will keep you on track and minimize stress along the way.

Remember, getting started is about laying the groundwork for a journey that will be filled with joy, challenges, and countless memorable moments. Your commitment to each other deserves to be celebrated in a way that feels authentic and true to your love story. So, let's embark on this chapter together, defining your vision, budgeting wisely, and setting a realistic timeline for the incredible adventure that lies ahead.

Defining Your Vision as a Couple

Your love story is a tapestry of unique moments, shared dreams, and the promise of a lifetime together. Now, as you step into the exciting world of wedding planning, the first and foremost task is to define your vision as a couple. This is not merely a checklist item; it's a heartfelt exploration that sets the stage for a celebration that authentically mirrors your love.

Start by having an open and honest conversation with your partner. What are the elements that make your relationship special? Reflect on the shared values, interests, and experiences that have woven the fabric of your connection. Your wedding day is an opportunity to showcase these elements, creating an atmosphere that feels deeply personal and true to who you are as a couple.

Consider the atmosphere and ambiance you envision for your celebration. Are you drawn to the idea of an intimate affair, surrounded by close friends and family? Or do you see yourselves hosting a grand celebration that reflects your vibrant energy and zest for life? Visualize the setting, the colors, and the overall vibe that resonates with both of you.

As you define your vision, also explore the concept of unity. How do you want to symbolize your commitment to each other? This could involve incorporating symbolic rituals or elements into your ceremony that hold personal significance. It's an opportunity to infuse your celebration with meaningful gestures that reflect the essence of your love story.

Your vision extends beyond the ceremony itself—it encompasses the entire experience. From the moment your guests receive the invitation to the final dance of the evening, every detail contributes to the narrative of your celebration. Think about the journey you want your guests to experience, from the first impression to the lasting memories they'll carry with them.

Engage in visual brainstorming together. Create mood boards, share Pinterest inspiration, or even jot down individual ideas that resonate. This collaborative approach not only strengthens your connection but also ensures that both partners feel represented in the vision-setting process.

Remember, there are no right or wrong answers when it comes to defining your vision. What matters most is that your celebration feels authentic and true to your relationship. This is your canvas, and you have the creative freedom to paint it with the hues of your love.

As you navigate the process of defining your vision, celebrate the uniqueness of your journey. This is the beginning of a beautiful adventure, and the choices you make now will lay the foundation for a wedding day that reflects the depth and authenticity of your love. So, let your hearts guide you, embrace the joy of envisioning your special day, and revel in the excitement of bringing your collective vision to life.

Budgeting Wisely for Your Dream Wedding

Embarking on the journey of wedding planning involves not only crafting a dream celebration but also navigating the practicalities of budgeting. While the prospect of creating a budget may seem daunting, it is, in fact, a liberating tool that empowers you to allocate resources wisely, ensuring that every dollar contributes meaningfully to your dream wedding.

Start by having an open and transparent conversation with your partner about your budgetary constraints and expectations. This initial dialogue sets the stage for a collaborative approach, where both partners feel involved in the decision-making process. Establishing a budget isn't about restriction; it's about making conscious choices that align with your financial goals and priorities.

Consider what aspects of the wedding hold the most significance for you. Whether it's the venue, the attire, or a specific element of the celebration, identifying your priorities allows you to allocate a larger portion of your budget to those areas. This ensures that the aspects most meaningful to you receive the attention and resources they deserve.

When creating your budget, factor in not just the major expenses but also the hidden or unexpected costs. It's the thoughtful consideration of these details that will prevent financial surprises and allow you to plan with confidence. From vendor tips to transportation and unforeseen expenses, a comprehensive budget accounts for every facet of your celebration.

Be realistic about your financial situation and set a budget that reflects your current reality. While it's natural to want the grandeur of a fairy-tale wedding, it's equally important to ensure that your celebration is financially responsible. Remember that a wedding is just the beginning of your journey together, and starting your life as a married couple with financial prudence sets a positive tone for the future.

Explore cost-saving strategies without compromising on the quality of your celebration. This could involve researching vendors, considering off-peak wedding dates, or exploring alternative options for certain aspects of your wedding. Creativity and flexibility are your allies in making the most of your budget.

Consider enlisting the help of a wedding planner who can assist in navigating the financial aspects of your celebration. Experienced wedding planners often have valuable insights, negotiation skills, and vendor relationships that can help stretch your budget without sacrificing your vision.

Throughout the budgeting process, keep in mind that unexpected expenses may arise. Building a contingency fund into your budget allows you to handle unforeseen circumstances with ease, providing a safety net for any surprises that may come your way.

Remember that your wedding is a celebration of love, and the significance of the day goes beyond financial considerations. While budgeting is a practical necessity, it's also an opportunity to be mindful of your priorities, make intentional choices, and create a celebration that feels both magical and financially responsible.

As you embark on the journey of budgeting for your dream wedding, celebrate the empowerment that comes with making conscious financial decisions. This process is not a restriction but rather a guide that allows you to allocate resources thoughtfully, ensuring that your wedding day is a reflection of your love story, your priorities, and your shared vision for the future. So, let's navigate this budgeting adventure together, with open hearts and a commitment to creating a celebration that is both dreamy and financially savvy.

Setting a Realistic Timeline for Planning

In the whirlwind of excitement that comes with planning a wedding, time becomes both your ally and your guide. Setting a realistic timeline is more than just a practical necessity; it's a thoughtful approach that allows you to navigate the myriad of decisions, big and small, with grace and ease. As you embark on this journey, consider your timeline not as a rigid schedule but as a flexible framework that embraces the joy of anticipation and the beauty of the planning process.

Start by envisioning your ideal wedding date. Is there a particular season, month, or even a significant day that holds special meaning for both of you? The choice of your wedding date is the cornerstone of your timeline and will influence many subsequent decisions. Be mindful of factors such as weather, availability of venues, and any personal or cultural considerations that may impact your preferred date.

Once you've established your wedding date, work backward to create a comprehensive timeline that covers every aspect of planning. The key is to strike a balance between having enough time to make thoughtful decisions and avoiding unnecessary stress from prolonged planning.

Begin with the major milestones. Booking your venue is often one of the first and most crucial steps. Popular venues can get booked well in advance, so securing your desired location early in the planning process ensures you have a solid foundation to build upon.

Consider the unique aspects of your celebration that may require additional time and attention. For example, if you're planning a destination wedding or incorporating intricate cultural traditions, allocate extra time to account for any logistical complexities.

As you navigate the timeline, embrace the joy of collaboration with your partner, families, and vendors. Building a team of professionals who share your vision and understand your timeline is invaluable.

Wedding planners, photographers, caterers—each plays a crucial role, and their expertise can guide you through the planning process with confidence.

Remember that flexibility is a key component of a realistic timeline. Unexpected circumstances may arise, and having a buffer allows you to navigate any challenges with ease. Be open to adjusting your timeline as needed, ensuring that the planning process remains an enjoyable and stress-free experience.

Communication is paramount throughout the planning journey. Regular check-ins with your partner, families, and vendors keep everyone on the same page and foster a collaborative spirit. Embrace the collective energy of your support team, drawing upon their expertise and insights as you progress through each phase of planning.

Celebrate the smaller victories along the way. Whether it's finalizing your guest list, selecting your attire, or tasting potential menu options, these milestones contribute to the overall tapestry of your wedding day. Acknowledge the joy in each decision, and let the planning process become a series of memorable moments leading up to the grand celebration.

Ultimately, your wedding timeline is a reflection of your unique journey. It's an unfolding story that captures the essence of your love, from the initial spark of inspiration to the triumphant moment you say, "I do." So, as you set a realistic timeline for planning, let it be a source of excitement, collaboration, and anticipation, guiding you through the adventure of crafting a celebration that is authentically yours.

Building Your Support Team

Welcome to Chapter 2: Building Your Support Team, a chapter that celebrates the strength found in connection and the power of shared enthusiasm as you embark on the exhilarating journey of wedding planning. Just as every great adventure is made richer by the companionship of fellow travelers, your wedding planning experience will be enhanced by the support of a dedicated team.

Your support team extends beyond the two of you, encompassing friends, family, and the professionals who will play a crucial role in bringing your dream celebration to life. In these pages, we explore the art of building a support system that not only understands your vision but also actively contributes to the joy and success of your wedding journey.

Assemble your wedding planning committee with intention, choosing individuals who not only bring unique perspectives but also share in the excitement of your union. Family members, close friends, or even a mentor who has experienced the joy of wedding planning—each member of your committee becomes a valuable voice, offering insights, advice, and, most importantly, unwavering encouragement.

Communication is the heartbeat of any support team. Regular check-ins with your committee create a collaborative atmosphere, ensuring that everyone is on the same page and that decisions are made collectively. Embrace the diversity of opinions within your team, recognizing that each perspective contributes to the richness of your planning experience.

Beyond your personal connections, tap into the wealth of resources offered by LGBTQ+ wedding communities and professionals. These networks provide a platform for shared experiences, advice, and inspiration tailored to the unique journey of same-sex couples. Engaging with these communities can be a source of both guidance and camaraderie, offering a sense of inclusivity that adds an extra layer of meaning to your celebration.

Your support team also includes the professionals who will turn your vision into reality. From wedding planners and photographers to caterers and florists, these individuals play a vital role in bringing the details of your celebration to life. Choose your vendors not only for their expertise but also for their passion and commitment to creating a celebration that aligns seamlessly with your vision.

In the chapters ahead, we'll delve into the dynamics of effective communication, collaboration, and decision-making within your support team. Together, let's navigate the art of building a network that uplifts, inspires, and stands with you as you craft a wedding day that not only celebrates your love but also reflects the strength and unity found in your chosen support system. So, let the journey continue, surrounded by the warmth and encouragement of those who champion your love story.

Assembling Your Wedding Planning Committee

The journey of wedding planning is an adventure best undertaken with the support of a dedicated team. Your wedding planning committee, often referred to as your "wedding squad," is a group of individuals who will play a pivotal role in shaping the narrative of your celebration. In this section, we explore the art of assembling a wedding planning committee that not only understands your vision but also contributes to the joy and success of your wedding journey.

Begin this process with an open and honest conversation with your partner. Consider your mutual connections, acknowledging the individuals who have been a consistent source of support and joy in your lives. Your committee should reflect the values and dynamics that are important to both of you, creating a diverse yet cohesive team that adds depth to the planning process.

Family members, close friends, and mentors can form the core of your wedding planning committee. Look for individuals who bring unique perspectives, talents, and experiences to the table. Their insights and advice will prove invaluable as you navigate the myriad decisions involved in planning your dream celebration.

When assembling your committee, it's crucial to choose individuals who not only share in the excitement of your union but also bring a positive and collaborative energy to the planning process. While differing opinions can contribute to a well-rounded perspective, a harmonious and supportive dynamic within your committee fosters an environment where creativity and joy can flourish.

Consider the strengths and talents of each committee member. Someone with a knack for organization might take on logistical aspects, while a friend with a keen eye for design could contribute to aesthetic decisions. The key is to leverage the unique skills of your committee members, allowing each person to play a role that aligns with their strengths and interests.

Effective communication is the glue that holds your committee together. Regular check-ins, whether through virtual meetings, phone calls, or in-person gatherings, ensure that everyone is on the same page and that decisions are made collaboratively. An open and transparent dialogue allows for the free exchange of ideas, creating a space where each committee member feels heard and valued.

Beyond your personal connections, consider tapping into LGBTQ+ wedding communities and online forums. These platforms offer a wealth of advice, shared experiences, and inspiration tailored to the unique journey of same-sex couples. Engaging with these communities can provide additional perspectives and a sense of inclusivity that enhances your planning experience.

As your wedding planning committee comes together, remember that this is not just a group of individuals helping plan a celebration—it's a support system that champions your love story. Celebrate the diversity within your committee, recognizing that each member contributes to the richness of your planning journey. Together, let your committee be a source of inspiration, laughter, and encouragement as you navigate the adventure of crafting a wedding day that is authentically yours.

Communicating Effectively with Family and Friends

Effective communication is the heartbeat of successful wedding planning, especially when it comes to interacting with family and friends. Your wedding is not only a celebration of your love but also a moment of shared joy with those closest to you. In this section, we explore the art of communication within the intricate tapestry of family dynamics and friendships, recognizing that open and transparent dialogue is key to a harmonious planning process.

Start by acknowledging that everyone involved has a unique perspective and their own set of expectations. Your wedding planning journey is an opportunity to build bridges, deepen connections, and foster understanding among family and friends. Approach conversations with an open heart and a willingness to listen, recognizing that effective communication is a two-way street.

Clearly articulate your vision as a couple. Share the elements that are most meaningful to you and explain how they contribute to the overall narrative of your celebration. Whether it's the choice of venue, the ceremony structure, or specific cultural elements, providing context helps your loved ones understand the thought and intention behind your decisions.

Be mindful of cultural and generational differences that may influence the expectations of family members. Wedding traditions and customs often carry significant meaning, and understanding these perspectives can pave the way for compromise and shared joy. Create a space where everyone feels comfortable expressing their thoughts, and seek common ground that respects both tradition and your unique vision.

When faced with differing opinions, approach the conversation with empathy and patience. Remember that everyone involved is invested in your happiness and the success of your celebration. Find common values and shared goals, emphasizing the love and unity that form the foundation of your wedding day.

For family members who may be new to the concept of same-sex weddings, take the opportunity to educate and share resources. Point them towards LGBTQ+ wedding communities, online forums, and real-life stories that showcase the diversity and beauty of same-sex unions. Encourage open-mindedness and let them see the love that transcends boundaries.

Maintain a balance between being assertive about your vision and being flexible to accommodate the wishes of family and friends. Sometimes, compromises can lead to unexpected and beautiful additions to your celebration. The key is to navigate these discussions with grace, creating an atmosphere of collaboration rather than confrontation.

As you communicate with your wedding planning committee, family, and friends, consider using technology to facilitate open dialogue. Virtual meetings, group chats, and shared online platforms provide convenient and accessible ways to keep everyone informed and engaged in the planning process. Leverage these tools to foster a sense of unity and shared excitement.

Throughout this communication journey, celebrate the victories, both big and small. Each conversation that deepens understanding, each compromise that fosters unity, contributes to the overall joy and success of your wedding planning experience. Let your communication be a reflection of the love that binds you not only as a couple but as a community of family and friends, all eager to contribute to the beauty of your celebration.

Tapping into LGBTQ+ Wedding Resources

In the vibrant tapestry of wedding planning, it's empowering to recognize that there is a wealth of LGBTQ+ wedding resources and communities ready to offer support, guidance, and inspiration. As you embark on the journey of crafting a celebration that authentically reflects your love story, tapping into these resources becomes a valuable tool in enhancing your planning experience.

Online LGBTQ+ wedding communities serve as virtual spaces where couples from diverse backgrounds share their experiences, advice, and triumphs. Engaging with these communities provides an opportunity to connect with others who have walked a similar path, offering insights and understanding that are uniquely tailored to the LGBTQ+ wedding journey.

Explore online forums, social media groups, and dedicated websites that focus on LGBTQ+ weddings. These platforms often feature real-life stories, practical advice, and discussions on various aspects of wedding planning. From navigating family dynamics to choosing LGBTQ+ inclusive vendors, these resources offer a wealth of knowledge that can help you make informed decisions throughout the planning process.

Consider attending LGBTQ+ wedding expos and events. These gatherings provide a unique space to connect with vendors, professionals, and other couples who share in the celebration of love. From photographers who specialize in capturing LGBTQ+ weddings to wedding planners with expertise in navigating the nuances of same-sex ceremonies, these events bring together a community that understands the intricacies of your journey.

Don't hesitate to reach out to LGBTQ+ couples who have already celebrated their weddings. Many couples are eager to share their experiences and offer guidance to those in the midst of planning. Whether through online forums or personal connections, building a network of individuals who have navigated the same path can be a source of inspiration and reassurance.

Explore LGBTQ+ wedding publications and blogs. These platforms showcase a diverse array of weddings, highlighting the creativity, love, and uniqueness that define same-sex celebrations. From styling inspiration to personal narratives, these resources offer a fresh perspective on wedding planning, allowing you to draw inspiration from a rich tapestry of LGBTQ+ love stories.

Consider incorporating LGBTQ+ symbolism and traditions into your celebration. Resources dedicated to LGBTQ+ weddings often provide insights into meaningful rituals and symbols that can be woven into the fabric of your ceremony. From incorporating pride colors into your wedding decor to exploring LGBTQ+ history, these elements add depth and significance to your celebration.

As you tap into LGBTQ+ wedding resources, approach the journey with an open heart and a willingness to embrace the diversity within the community. Each love story is unique, and these resources serve as a guide that respects and celebrates the individuality of same-sex unions. Whether you're seeking advice on inclusive language for your invitations or exploring LGBTQ+ friendly honeymoon destinations, these resources are here to support you at every step.

Ultimately, the beauty of tapping into LGBTQ+ wedding resources lies in the shared understanding and celebration of love in all its forms. Let these platforms be a source of inspiration, knowledge, and connection as you navigate the adventure of planning a wedding that is authentically and unequivocally yours.

Selecting the Perfect Venue

Welcome to Chapter 3: Selecting the Perfect Venue, a chapter that unveils the canvas upon which your love story will be painted—a canvas as diverse and unique as the journey that brought you together. Choosing the ideal venue is a pivotal step in your wedding planning adventure, setting the stage for a celebration that resonates with your personalities, preferences, and the collective energy of your love.

In the pages ahead, we'll navigate the intricacies of venue selection, exploring the factors that transform a space into a place of meaningful significance. Your wedding venue is more than a backdrop; it's a character in the narrative of your love, influencing the atmosphere, aesthetic, and overall experience of your celebration.

Begin this exploration by envisioning the atmosphere you desire for your wedding day. Do you dream of an intimate garden ceremony, a sophisticated ballroom affair, or perhaps a destination celebration that reflects your adventurous spirit? Your venue becomes the backdrop to these dreams, and the choices are as boundless as the love that brings you together.

Consider the logistical aspects of each potential venue, from the number of guests it can comfortably accommodate to its accessibility for loved ones. Your venue should not only align with your vision but also provide a seamless experience for everyone present, allowing them to focus on the joyous moments of your celebration.

Throughout this chapter, we'll delve into the nuances of venue selection, offering insights into the questions to ask, the details to consider, and the hidden gems that can elevate your chosen space. Whether you're drawn to a historic landmark, a rustic barn, or a modern urban setting, each venue presents its own set of possibilities, and we're here to guide you in making the choice that feels like the perfect embodiment of your love story.

As you embark on this chapter, let your hearts be open to the magic of discovery. Your perfect venue is not just a physical space; it's a place where love blossoms, laughter echoes, and memories are etched into the very walls. So, join us in the exploration of selecting the perfect venue—a journey that leads you to a place where your love takes center stage, surrounded by the warmth and beauty of a space that feels uniquely yours.

Exploring LGBTQ+-Friendly Wedding Destinations

Your wedding destination is not just a location; it's a statement of love, an expression of your unique journey, and an opportunity to celebrate in a place that resonates with your shared spirit. In this section, we embark on the exciting exploration of LGBTQ+-friendly wedding destinations, recognizing that the world is filled with enchanting locales ready to embrace and elevate your celebration.

Choosing a destination for your wedding involves a delightful balance between personal preferences and the welcoming nature of the locale. Many destinations worldwide have become known for their LGBTQ+ inclusivity, creating an atmosphere where love knows no boundaries.

Consider cities that have established themselves as LGBTQ+ havens, celebrating diversity and fostering a sense of inclusivity. From the vibrant neighborhoods of San Francisco to the iconic canals of Amsterdam, these destinations not only provide a stunning backdrop but also offer a community that understands and celebrates the beauty of same-sex unions.

Destination weddings often conjure images of tropical paradises, and many such locales are not only picturesque but also known for their LGBTQ+-friendly atmospheres. Imagine exchanging vows on a sun-kissed beach in Puerto Vallarta, dancing under the stars in Mykonos, or having an intimate ceremony in the lush landscapes of Costa Rica. These destinations offer not only natural beauty but also a warmth and acceptance that enhances the joy of your celebration.

Explore countries that have embraced marriage equality, creating a legal framework that recognizes and validates same-sex unions. Whether it's the stunning landscapes of New Zealand, the historic charm of South Africa, or the romantic allure of Canada, these destinations not only offer breathtaking settings but also ensure that your marriage is legally recognized, providing an additional layer of significance to your celebration.

While some couples may be drawn to the energy of bustling cities, others may find solace in the tranquility of more secluded destinations. From the majestic beauty of the Swiss Alps to the serene beaches of Bali, the choices are as diverse as the couples who choose them. Your wedding destination is a reflection of your personalities and the unique connection you share.

When exploring LGBTQ+-friendly wedding destinations, consider reaching out to local wedding planners and vendors who are experienced in catering to same-sex couples. Their expertise can be invaluable in navigating the logistics of a destination wedding, ensuring that your celebration is not only visually stunning but also seamlessly executed.

Beyond the logistics, immerse yourselves in the local culture and traditions of your chosen destination. Whether it's incorporating regional cuisine into your wedding menu, embracing local customs in your ceremony, or even having a pre-wedding photoshoot at iconic landmarks, these experiences add depth and authenticity to your celebration.

As you embark on the journey of exploring LGBTQ+-friendly wedding destinations, let your hearts be open to the possibilities that each locale presents. Your wedding destination is more than just a place; it's a destination of love, acceptance, and celebration. So, let the exploration begin, and may you find a destination that not only captures the essence of your love story but also becomes a canvas for the beautiful tapestry of your wedding day.

Navigating Traditional and Non-Traditional Spaces

The choice of your wedding venue is a profound decision, setting the stage for the unfolding chapters of your love story. In this section, we explore the nuanced journey of navigating traditional and non-traditional spaces, recognizing that the perfect venue is not bound by conventions but rather shaped by the authenticity of your connection.

Traditional wedding venues, such as grand ballrooms, historic estates, and elegant hotels, often carry a timeless allure. These spaces provide a classic backdrop, allowing couples to embrace the grace of tradition while infusing the celebration with their unique flair. The grandeur of a historic ballroom or the charm of a centuries-old estate can create an atmosphere of sophistication and refinement, offering a canvas for couples who appreciate the beauty of tradition.

Non-traditional spaces, on the other hand, invite couples to think beyond the expected, exploring venues that defy convention and provide a blank canvas for creative expression. Warehouses, art galleries, botanical gardens, and even rooftop spaces offer an opportunity to craft a celebration that reflects your personalities and challenges the boundaries of tradition. These venues often provide a more versatile setting, allowing couples to shape the space in a way that aligns with their vision.

When navigating traditional spaces, consider how you can infuse your unique style into the established aesthetic. Personalize the venue with touches that speak to your love story, whether it's custom decor, meaningful symbolism, or cultural elements that hold significance. Traditional spaces become a canvas for your creativity, allowing you to honor tradition while making the celebration distinctly yours.

Non-traditional spaces offer a playground of possibilities, encouraging couples to think outside the box and embrace the unexpected. The raw and industrial ambiance of a warehouse, for example, can be transformed into a bohemian wonderland with the right decor and lighting. Botanical gardens provide a natural setting for an outdoor celebration, while art galleries offer a contemporary backdrop for couples with a flair for the avant-garde.

Consider the logistical aspects of each venue, regardless of its traditional or non-traditional nature. Accessibility, capacity, and amenities are key factors that influence the overall experience for you and your guests. Whether you choose a historic mansion or an intimate garden, ensuring that the venue aligns with your practical needs contributes to a seamless and enjoyable celebration.

Navigating traditional and non-traditional spaces is not about adhering to a set of rules but rather about selecting a venue that feels like an extension of your love story. It's about finding a space that resonates with your vision and creates an atmosphere where your personalities can shine. As you explore venues, keep in mind that the perfect space is the one that feels right for you—a place where you can envision your love story unfolding and where every detail reflects the depth and authenticity of your connection.

Whether you choose a centuries-old chapel, an art-filled loft, or a rustic barn, let the venue be a reflection of your journey. The beauty of navigating traditional and non-traditional spaces lies in the freedom to choose a setting that celebrates your love in all its unique glory. So, let the exploration begin, and may you discover a venue that not only captures the essence of your story but also becomes a cherished part of the beautiful tapestry of your wedding day.

Considering Cultural and Religious Influences

The choice of a wedding venue is a deeply personal decision, one that often intertwines with cultural and religious influences. In this section, we delve into the enriching journey of considering these influences, recognizing that the venue becomes not just a backdrop but a space where tradition, spirituality, and personal expression converge.

Cultural and religious elements add a profound layer of significance to the wedding ceremony and celebration. Whether you are rooted in specific cultural traditions or follow religious practices, these influences shape the narrative of your wedding day, creating a tapestry of meaning and connection.

For couples with strong cultural ties, selecting a venue that aligns with these traditions can be a deeply meaningful choice. This might involve choosing a venue that resonates with the architectural styles or historical significance of your cultural background. For example, a couple with South Asian heritage might opt for a venue adorned with vibrant colors and intricate designs to complement the richness of their cultural traditions.

Religious influences often guide the choice of venues, particularly for couples who wish to incorporate specific religious rituals into their ceremony. Churches, synagogues, temples, and mosques provide sacred spaces where couples can receive blessings, exchange vows, and honor the spiritual aspects of their union. These venues often carry a sense of reverence and tradition, offering a setting that reflects the couple's faith and commitment.

When considering cultural and religious influences in venue selection, it's important to strike a balance between honoring tradition and expressing your unique identity as a couple. Some couples may choose to incorporate cultural elements into a more neutral venue, allowing for a fusion of traditions. Others may opt for a venue that is inherently tied to their cultural or religious background, creating a seamless integration of tradition into every aspect of the celebration.

Communication plays a crucial role in this journey. Discuss with your partner and families about the cultural and religious aspects that hold significance for you. Seek venues that not only accommodate these influences but also provide a supportive and understanding atmosphere. Many venues, regardless of their primary style, are experienced in hosting diverse cultural and religious celebrations and may offer flexibility to customize the space according to your needs.

Consider the logistics of incorporating cultural and religious influences into your chosen venue. Whether it's the placement of ceremonial items, the accommodation of specific rituals, or the availability of religious officiants, these details contribute to the seamless integration of tradition into your celebration.

As you navigate the terrain of cultural and religious influences, remember that the perfect venue is one that allows you to authentically express your identity as a couple. It's a space where tradition and personalization coexist, creating an atmosphere that is not only rich in cultural and religious significance but also a true reflection of your love story.

Ultimately, the journey of considering cultural and religious influences in venue selection is an opportunity to celebrate the diversity of your backgrounds and the shared values that form the foundation of your union. Whether you choose a venue steeped in tradition or one that offers a more neutral canvas for customization, let the choice be a celebration of your unique journey—a space where culture, religion, and love converge in a harmonious celebration of your commitment.

Crafting Your Unique Ceremony

Welcome to Chapter 4: Crafting Your Unique Ceremony, where the pages unfold into a space of creativity, intention, and profound connection. Your wedding ceremony is the heartbeat of your celebration, a moment when time stands still, and the essence of your love is woven into the fabric of eternity. In this chapter, we embark on a journey that transcends tradition, inviting you to embrace the power of personalization and craft a ceremony that reflects the unique tapestry of your love story.

Your wedding ceremony is a canvas waiting to be painted with the strokes of your individuality. As you step into the realm of crafting this pivotal moment, let your hearts guide the way, and allow the ceremony to be a reflection of the shared dreams, values, and promises that define your journey as a couple.

Gone are the days of one-size-fits-all ceremonies. In these pages, we explore the art of infusing your ceremony with the authenticity that makes it distinctly yours. Whether you're drawn to time-honored traditions, cultural rituals, or envision a ceremony that defies conventions, the possibilities are as limitless as your love.

As you delve into the process of crafting your unique ceremony, consider the elements that hold personal significance. Is there a reading that resonates with the depths of your connection? Do you wish to include cultural rituals that honor your heritage? Perhaps you envision writing your own vows, allowing the words spoken in that moment to be a testament to the unique bond you share.

This chapter is not a guide to the "right" way to conduct a ceremony but an exploration of the myriad ways you can make it yours. From the choice of officiant to the selection of music, every decision is an opportunity to infuse your ceremony with the spirit of your love. Let your personalities shine through, and let the ceremony be a reflection of the love that has brought you to this profound moment.

Crafting Your Unique Ceremony is an invitation to embrace the freedom to be wholly yourselves. It's a celebration of the quirks, the inside jokes, and the shared glances that define your connection. So, as you turn the pages and venture into the heart of crafting your ceremony, may you find inspiration, guidance, and the joy of creating a moment that resonates with the very essence of your love story.

Designing Personalized Vows

Your wedding vows are the whispered promises that linger in the air, binding your hearts in a sacred commitment. In this section, we explore the art of designing personalized vows—a journey that goes beyond traditional scripts and invites you to articulate the depth of your love in words that are uniquely yours.

Personalized vows are a canvas for self-expression, a moment in the ceremony where you lay bare the intimate truths of your hearts. Begin this creative process by reflecting on the essence of your relationship. What unique qualities define your connection? What promises do you wish to make to each other as you embark on this journey of marriage?

Consider the tone of your vows. Whether you choose to infuse them with humor, poetic language, or heartfelt simplicity, let the tone align with your personalities and the atmosphere you wish to create during the ceremony. Some couples find joy in injecting humor, sharing anecdotes that celebrate the quirks of their relationship. Others prefer a more poetic and romantic expression, crafting vows that resonate with the timeless beauty of their love story.

In your vows, acknowledge the journey that has brought you to this moment. Share the milestones, challenges, and growth you've experienced together. This is an opportunity to celebrate not just the present moment but the entire tapestry of your shared history. Let the vows be a testament to the resilience and strength of your love.

Include promises that reflect the values and aspirations you hold as a couple. Whether it's a commitment to support each other's dreams, to navigate challenges with grace, or to continue growing together, let your promises be a reflection of the unique bond you share. Your vows are a covenant that defines the path you choose to walk together.

Craft your vows with intention and authenticity. Speak from the heart, using words that resonate with the depth of your emotions. Avoid clichés or generic phrases and instead, focus on expressing your love in a way that feels genuine and true to your connection. Remember, there is no right or wrong way to design your vows; what matters is that they authentically represent the love you share.

Consider incorporating shared experiences, inside jokes, or meaningful references into your vows. These personal touches add a layer of intimacy to the ceremony, creating a moment that is not only witnessed by your loved ones but is a true reflection of the unique language and history you've built together.

Practice saying your vows aloud to gauge the flow and ensure that they are comfortable to speak. This process not only familiarizes you with the words but also allows you to fine-tune the delivery, ensuring that the vows resonate with the emotional depth you wish to convey.

In the end, designing personalized vows is a deeply personal and creative endeavor. It's an opportunity to infuse your ceremony with the authenticity of your love and to create a moment that will be etched into the memories of all who bear witness. So, as you embark on this journey of crafting vows, may your words be a celebration of the profound connection you share—a promise that echoes with the uniqueness of your love story.

Selecting Meaningful Rituals and Traditions

In the tapestry of wedding ceremonies, rituals and traditions are the threads that weave depth and significance into the fabric of the celebration. In this exploration, we delve into the art of selecting meaningful rituals and traditions—a journey that invites you to honor your heritage, embrace symbolism, and infuse your ceremony with timeless gestures that resonate with the essence of your love.

Start this journey by reflecting on your cultural background and personal experiences. Consider the rituals and traditions that hold deep meaning for you, whether rooted in your cultural heritage, family customs, or shared beliefs. This exploration is an opportunity to celebrate the richness of your identity and weave these elements into the very fabric of your ceremony.

For couples with diverse cultural backgrounds, this is a chance to create a fusion of traditions, honoring each heritage in a way that feels authentic and harmonious. Consider blending elements of your respective cultures, incorporating rituals that hold personal significance for both of you. This not only celebrates the diversity within your relationship but also creates a unique ceremony that reflects the union of two distinct worlds.

Explore rituals that symbolize unity, commitment, and the journey of your relationship. The unity candle, where two flames become one, represents the merging of two lives into a shared journey. The sand ceremony, where different colored sands are combined, signifies the blending of individual paths into a singular, harmonious existence. Choose a ritual that resonates with you and captures the essence of your commitment.

Consider rituals that involve your families or close friends, creating a sense of communal celebration. The breaking of the glass in Jewish ceremonies, the exchange of flower garlands in Hindu weddings, or the binding of hands in a handfasting ceremony are all examples of rituals that involve loved ones, symbolizing the support and connection that surround your union.

Personalize traditional rituals to make them uniquely yours. Whether it's a cultural tradition passed down through generations or a ceremony inspired by your favorite book, movie, or shared passion, infuse your ceremony with elements that speak to the very heart of your connection. Let your creativity and individuality shine through, transforming timeless rituals into moments that feel deeply personal.

Consider rituals that honor the natural world and the elements. An outdoor ceremony might include an earth blessing, where soil from meaningful locations is combined, or a tree-planting ceremony to symbolize growth and resilience. Embracing the elements adds a touch of nature's poetry to your celebration, creating a connection to the world around you.

Before incorporating a ritual, take the time to understand its significance and the cultural or religious context from which it originates. This ensures that the ritual is performed with respect and understanding, allowing it to authentically contribute to the overall meaning of your ceremony.

In the end, selecting meaningful rituals and traditions is an invitation to infuse your ceremony with layers of significance. It's a journey that celebrates the beauty of diversity, the richness of cultural heritage, and the uniqueness of your love story. As you embark on this exploration, may the rituals you choose become not just moments within the ceremony but timeless expressions of the love that binds you together—a celebration of the past, present, and future that unfolds in the sacred space of your wedding day.

Incorporating LGBTQ+ Symbolism

Your wedding ceremony is a canvas for personal expression, an opportunity to celebrate the unique aspects of your love story. In this exploration, we delve into the meaningful journey of incorporating LGBTQ+ symbolism—a tapestry of colors, symbols, and gestures that reflect the diversity and beauty of your relationship.

Start by considering the colors that hold significance within the LGBTQ+ community. The rainbow flag, with its vibrant spectrum of colors, is a powerful symbol of pride, unity, and inclusion. Incorporating these colors into your ceremony can be a visually stunning way to celebrate your identity and the broader LGBTQ+ community. Whether it's through decor, attire, or floral arrangements, let the rainbow colors become a joyful expression of your love.

The use of the rainbow flag extends beyond colors; each stripe holds its own significance. Red represents life, orange symbolizes healing, yellow embodies sunlight, green signifies nature, blue represents harmony, and purple represents spirit. Consider how these individual meanings can be woven into the narrative of your ceremony, allowing each color to carry its own significance.

Explore symbols that resonate with the LGBTQ+ community and hold personal meaning for you as a couple. The lambda symbol, derived from the Greek alphabet, has been embraced as a symbol of LGBTQ+ rights and liberation. Incorporating the lambda into your ceremony, whether through decor or accessories, is a subtle yet powerful nod to the community's history and ongoing fight for equality.

Consider incorporating the pink triangle, which holds a poignant historical significance. Originally used as a symbol of persecution during the Holocaust, the pink triangle has been reclaimed by the LGBTQ+ community as a symbol of resilience and pride. Including this symbol in your ceremony is a way to honor the struggles of the past while celebrating the strength and triumphs of the present.

Incorporate LGBTQ+ symbolism into your attire or accessories. Lapel pins, jewelry, or even socks in rainbow colors or featuring LGBTQ+ symbols can be subtle yet impactful ways to express your identity. These personal touches not only add a layer of meaning to your attire but also create a visual connection to the broader LGBTQ+ community.

Consider a ritual that symbolizes the unity and equality within your relationship. The exchange of rainbow-colored rings, the lighting of unity candles in the colors of the LGBTQ+ flag, or a handfasting ceremony with rainbow-colored ribbons are all beautiful ways to incorporate symbolism into the ceremony itself. These rituals become tangible expressions of your commitment and celebration of LGBTQ+ love.

Artistic expressions, such as custom illustrations or paintings featuring LGBTQ+ symbols, can serve as lasting reminders of your love story. Consider commissioning artwork that incorporates meaningful symbols, colors, and elements that hold significance for both of you. This unique piece of art becomes a representation of your love and a cherished memento of your wedding day.

Incorporating LGBTQ+ symbolism is not just about visual aesthetics; it's about infusing your ceremony with layers of meaning that resonate with your identity and the broader LGBTQ+ community. Whether you choose subtle nods or bold expressions, let the symbolism be a celebration of the love that transcends boundaries—a love that is as diverse and beautiful as the colors of the rainbow. As you weave these symbols into the fabric of your ceremony, may they become not just gestures but profound expressions of pride, love, and the shared journey that defines your union.

CHAPTER 5

Dressing for the Occasion

Welcome to Chapter 5: Dressing for the Occasion, where the threads of style, individuality, and the essence of your love story come together in a celebration of sartorial expression. Your wedding attire is more than fabric and design; it's a reflection of your personalities, a nod to tradition, and a canvas for the unique narrative of your commitment. In this chapter, we embark on a journey into the world of wedding fashion—a realm where attire becomes a visual language, speaking volumes about the love you share.

Choosing what to wear on your wedding day is a decision that goes beyond the aesthetic—it's about capturing the spirit of your love and expressing it through your clothing. This chapter is not a guide to trends or a rulebook on fashion etiquette; it's an exploration of the possibilities that await as you select attire that feels authentic and true to the essence of your relationship.

As you step into the realm of dressing for the occasion, consider the nuances of your personal style. Whether you lean towards timeless elegance, bohemian flair, or contemporary chic, let your attire be an extension of the fashion language you both speak. This is an opportunity to celebrate your individuality and create a cohesive look that resonates with the collective energy of your union.

For many couples, wedding attire becomes a bridge between tradition and personal expression. Whether you choose to honor cultural heritage through specific garments, infuse LGBTQ+ pride into your wardrobe, or create a fusion of styles that reflects your diverse backgrounds, the attire becomes a living testament to the beautiful tapestry of your love story.

In the chapters ahead, we'll explore the intricacies of wedding fashion, from choosing the perfect wedding gown or suit to coordinating attire with your partner. Whether you're drawn to classic white or envision a burst of color, navigating the world of accessories, or exploring LGBTQ+-inclusive designers, this chapter is a guide through the myriad choices that await you on your journey to dressing for the occasion.

Beyond the aesthetics, we'll delve into the practical aspects of wedding attire, offering insights into the importance of comfort, choosing attire that complements your venue, and making decisions that align with the vision you have for your celebration. The attire you choose becomes a part of the memories you create on your wedding day, and this chapter is here to help you make choices that feel not only stylish but deeply meaningful.

So, as you turn the pages of Chapter 6, may you find inspiration, guidance, and the joy of discovering the perfect ensemble that encapsulates the essence of your love. Whether you're envisioning classic fairytale attire, a sleek and modern suit, or something entirely unique, let your wedding attire be a reflection of the love that binds you together—a visual testament to the beauty of your commitment as you step into the spotlight of your wedding day.

Navigating Men's Wedding Fashion Trends

The world of men's wedding fashion is a delightful spectrum of style, offering an array of choices that allow you to express your personality and make a statement on your special day. As you embark on this journey, navigating through trends, cuts, and fabrics, remember that your wedding attire is a canvas—a reflection of the unique love story you share with your partner.

Classic Elegance:

For those who appreciate timeless sophistication, classic wedding attire continues to hold a timeless allure. A well-tailored black or navy suit remains a perennial favorite, exuding an air of refined elegance. Consider experimenting with subtle details like a peak lapel or a silk-lined jacket to add a touch of individuality to the traditional silhouette.

Contemporary Chic:

Modern grooms are increasingly gravitating towards contemporary styles that embrace sleek lines and minimalist aesthetics. Slim-fit suits or tuxedos in shades like charcoal, gray, or even deep burgundy are popular choices. Experiment with unconventional details, such as a textured fabric or a contrasting lapel, to inject a contemporary twist into your wedding ensemble.

Bohemian Vibes:

For those envisioning a more relaxed and bohemian aesthetic, explore the world of boho-inspired wedding fashion. Lighter fabrics like linen or cotton suits in earthy tones provide a laid-back yet stylish look. Consider adding personal touches like a patterned shirt or a unique tie to infuse your ensemble with bohemian charm.

Bold Colors:

The traditional black and white palette has given way to a spectrum of bold colors for men's wedding fashion. Deep blues, rich greens, and even shades of red or burgundy are making a splash. These colors not only add vibrancy to your ensemble but also offer the opportunity to make a bold and memorable statement on your wedding day.

Mix and Match:

Embrace the trend of mix-and-match suits, allowing you to create a personalized and eclectic look. Consider pairing different colored jackets and trousers for a playful yet sophisticated appearance. This approach not only allows you to showcase your creativity but also ensures that your attire is uniquely yours.

Accessories Matter:

Elevate your wedding attire with carefully chosen accessories that reflect your style. A well-chosen tie, pocket square, or boutonniere can add a pop of color and personality to your ensemble. Experiment with textures and patterns to create visual interest and make your attire truly stand out.

Fit is Key:

Regardless of the style you choose, the fit of your wedding attire is paramount. A well-fitted suit enhances your silhouette and ensures you feel confident and comfortable throughout the day. Consider seeking the expertise of a skilled tailor to achieve a personalized fit that complements your body shape.

As you navigate men's wedding fashion trends, let your choices be guided by your personal style, the overall theme of your celebration, and, most importantly, the connection you share with your partner. Whether you opt for a timeless classic, a contemporary chic look, or a bohemian-inspired ensemble, your wedding attire is a celebration of your love—a visual expression of the beautiful union you're about to embark upon. So, as you explore the world of men's wedding fashion, may you find inspiration, confidence, and the perfect ensemble that speaks to the unique narrative of your love story.

Choosing Attire that Reflects Your Personal Style

Your wedding day is a canvas for self-expression, and your attire plays a starring role in telling the story of your unique love. As you stand on the threshold of choosing the perfect wedding attire, the guiding principle should be authenticity—let your personal style shine through every fabric, stitch, and detail.

Begin this exploration by delving into your everyday wardrobe. What styles, colors, and fabrics resonate with your personality? Your wedding attire is an extension of your daily fashion sensibilities, so start with what feels familiar and true to you. If you're someone who gravitates towards classic styles, a timeless suit in a neutral hue may be the perfect fit.

For those with a penchant for contemporary trends, explore sleek cuts, unconventional colors, or modern accessories to add a touch of flair.

Consider the narrative you wish to convey through your attire. Your wedding ensemble is not merely clothing; it's a visual language that communicates the essence of your relationship. If your love story is steeped in tradition, explore ways to infuse cultural or familial elements into your attire. Embroidered details, symbolic accessories, or a specific color palette can honor your heritage while allowing you to express your personal style.

For the free spirits who embrace a bohemian lifestyle, wedding fashion offers endless possibilities. Flowing fabrics, earthy tones, and relaxed silhouettes can create a boho-inspired look that feels both effortless and stylish.

Remember that comfort is the cornerstone of confidence. Whether you're opting for a suit, tuxedo, or a more casual ensemble, prioritize comfort without compromising style. A well-fitted suit that allows you to move with ease ensures that you not only look good but also feel good on your wedding day.

Experiment with color to make a statement that is uniquely yours. While classic black and navy suits exude timeless elegance, don't hesitate to explore a broader palette. Deep burgundies, rich greens, or even unconventional shades like mustard or dusty blue can add a personal touch to your attire. The color you choose can be symbolic, reflect your personality, or simply be a nod to the overall theme of your celebration.

Your wedding attire is a collaborative effort. Discuss your choices with your partner to ensure a cohesive look that reflects both your individual styles and the collective vision for the day. Coordination doesn't necessarily mean matching outfits; it's about creating a harmonious aesthetic that complements each other's choices.

Lastly, trust your instincts. Wedding fashion may come with its trends and guidelines, but the ultimate authority on what you should wear is you. If you feel a connection to a certain style, color, or accessory, embrace it. Your wedding day is a celebration of your love, and your attire is a manifestation of that celebration—so let it be a true reflection of you.

In the realm of choosing attire that reflects your personal style, there are no rules, only possibilities. So, as you navigate the journey of selecting the perfect ensemble, let it be an adventure of self-discovery, authenticity, and celebration. May your wedding attire not only make a statement about your love but also be a testament to the beautifully unique individuals who are about to embark on a lifelong journey together.

Exploring Options for Wedding Party Attire

As you plan your wedding day, the attire of your wedding party becomes a canvas to paint a cohesive and visually stunning picture. Whether you're envisioning a traditional wedding party, a mixed-gender lineup, or an inclusive celebration with friends and family, exploring options for wedding party attire is an exciting journey that adds a layer of style and harmony to your overall aesthetic.

Start by considering the overall theme and style of your wedding. The attire of your wedding party should complement the vibe you wish to create. For a formal affair, classic suits and elegant gowns may be the perfect fit. If you're leaning towards a more casual or bohemian celebration, consider relaxed styles, mix-and-match ensembles, or even attire that incorporates elements of your chosen theme.

Coordination doesn't necessarily mean identical outfits. Embrace the trend of mix-and-match attire, allowing each member of your wedding party to express their individual style while maintaining a cohesive look. Consider a consistent color palette, a unifying accessory, or a shared detail that ties the ensembles together. This approach not only adds visual interest but also allows your wedding party to feel comfortable and authentic in their chosen attire.

Explore a variety of styles that accommodate diverse preferences and body types. For bridesmaids, consider offering different dress styles in the same color or fabric, allowing each member to choose a silhouette that suits their figure and style. Groomsmen can experiment with variations in suit cuts, tie styles, or even the choice of accessories to create a unified yet personalized look.

Inclusivity is key, especially if your wedding party includes members of different genders or non-binary individuals. The idea is to create an environment where everyone feels comfortable and celebrated. This may involve offering a range of attire options that cater to diverse gender expressions or encouraging the wedding party to choose attire that aligns with their individual styles.

Think beyond traditional roles and explore creative alternatives. Some couples choose to forgo a strict bridal party and instead invite close friends and family to wear attire that aligns with the overall theme. This not only fosters inclusivity but also allows for a more relaxed and enjoyable atmosphere.

Consider the comfort and preferences of your wedding party members. While aesthetics are important, ensuring that everyone feels comfortable and confident in their attire is equally crucial. Take into account factors like the weather, venue, and any specific cultural or religious considerations that may influence the choice of attire.

Remember that your wedding party attire sets the tone for the celebration. Whether you opt for timeless classics, contemporary chic, or a more eclectic mix-and-match approach, the goal is to create a visually cohesive and harmonious ensemble that adds to the overall beauty of your wedding day.

Communication is key when exploring options for wedding party attire. Keep an open dialogue with your wedding party members, share your vision, and encourage them to express their preferences. A collaborative approach ensures that everyone feels heard and valued, contributing to a positive and enjoyable experience for all.

In the realm of wedding party attire, there are endless possibilities to explore. Whether you're aiming for a polished and traditional look or embracing a more relaxed and eclectic vibe, let the attire of your wedding party be a reflection of the joy, diversity, and shared celebration that defines your special day. As you embark on this exploration, may the attire of your wedding party become not just an ensemble but a collective expression of the love and camaraderie that surrounds your union.

Invitations and Guest Management

Welcome to Chapter 6: Invitations and Guest Management, the gateway to the heart of your wedding celebration. The invitations you send and the way you manage your guest list are more than logistical details—they're the first glimpse your loved ones have into the magic and uniqueness of your upcoming union. In this chapter, we embark on a journey into the world of wedding invitations and guest management, where every detail is an opportunity to extend a warm welcome and set the tone for the joyous celebration that awaits.

Your wedding invitations are more than pieces of paper; they're emissaries of love, carrying the essence of your commitment to every recipient. As you peruse the vast array of designs, fonts, and styles, remember that these invitations are the prelude to the story you're about to unfold—a story of love, connection, and the shared moments that will become cherished memories.

The process of creating and sending invitations is a unique chance to infuse your personality into every envelope. Whether you opt for elegant and formal, playful and whimsical, or something entirely unconventional, let your invitations be a reflection of the love that binds you and the celebration you're planning.

Beyond the aesthetics, managing your guest list is a delicate dance of considerations. Who will witness your vows, share in the laughter, and dance the night away with you? This chapter guides you through the intricacies of crafting a guest list that balances your vision, venue capacity, and the desire to share your special day with those who matter most.

We'll delve into the art of crafting invitations that not only convey the essential details but also evoke the spirit of your celebration. Whether you're going digital, exploring intricate paper designs, or adding personalized touches, the goal is to create invitations that your guests will treasure and that will build anticipation for the joyous occasion ahead.

Guest management extends beyond the act of sending invitations. It involves navigating RSVPs, accommodating dietary preferences, and ensuring that every guest feels seen and valued. We'll explore strategies for effective guest communication, thoughtful seating arrangements, and other considerations that contribute to a seamless and enjoyable experience for everyone attending.

As you navigate the realms of invitations and guest management, remember that these details are the threads weaving your loved ones into the fabric of your celebration. Every name on your guest list is a chapter in the story of your union, and every invitation is an invitation to share in the love that binds you.

So, as you turn the pages of Chapter 7, may you find inspiration, guidance, and the joy of extending a warm welcome to those who will play a part in the beautiful tapestry of your wedding day. Whether you're sending out whimsical invites or crafting an intimate guest list, let this chapter be your companion in the art of inviting and managing the guests who will witness and celebrate the unfolding chapters of your love story.

Designing LGBTQ+-Inclusive Invitations

Your wedding invitations are not just a formality; they are an expression of your love story, and their design holds the power to convey inclusivity, diversity, and the unique nature of your relationship. In this section, we explore the art of designing LGBTQ+-inclusive invitations—a journey into creativity, symbolism, and thoughtful details that speak to the heart of your celebration.

The foundation of LGBTQ+ inclusivity in wedding invitations lies in the language used. Ensure that your invitations are gender-neutral, using terms like "together with their families" or "celebrating their union" instead of gender-specific language. This not only reflects the inclusivity of your celebration but also sets an open and welcoming tone for your guests.

Consider incorporating LGBTQ+ symbolism into your invitations. The rainbow flag, a universally recognized symbol of LGBTQ+ pride, can be subtly integrated into the design or color palette. Whether it's through a spectrum of colors, a discreet rainbow accent, or even using the flag itself in a creative way, these symbols add layers of meaning that resonate with the LGBTQ+ community.

Explore diverse representations in the illustrations or graphics used in your invitations. Traditional depictions of wedding couples often default to heteronormative imagery, but your invitations can challenge and expand these norms. Consider custom illustrations that represent diverse gender expressions and relationships, ensuring that every guest sees a reflection of love that mirrors the beautiful diversity of the LGBTQ+ community.

Play with color schemes that go beyond traditional wedding palettes. While classic whites and pastels are timeless, don't hesitate to experiment with vibrant and bold colors that reflect the vibrancy of LGBTQ+ celebrations. Consider incorporating the colors of the transgender pride flag, bisexual pride flag, or other meaningful palettes that resonate with your identity or community.

Think beyond binary distinctions in RSVP cards and other wedding stationery. Instead of the traditional "Mr." and "Mrs." titles, opt for gender-neutral options like "Mx." or omit titles altogether. This small but impactful detail communicates a commitment to inclusivity and acknowledges the diverse identities of your guests.

Include quotes, poems, or verses that celebrate love in all its forms. This could be a line from a LGBTQ+ poet, an excerpt from a same-sex love story, or a universally resonant quote that captures the essence of your commitment. These words become more than just text on paper; they become a declaration of love that transcends boundaries.

Consider offering options for attire suggestions that accommodate various gender expressions. Instead of adhering strictly to "black-tie" or "formal," provide guidance that allows guests to express their individual styles comfortably. This flexibility not only reflects inclusivity but also fosters an environment where everyone feels celebrated for who they are.

In the design process, collaborate with LGBTQ+-inclusive vendors who understand the nuances and sensitivities of creating invitations that truly represent your love story. Seek out designers, illustrators, and printers who are experienced in crafting LGBTQ+-inclusive wedding stationery and can bring your vision to life with authenticity and respect.

Designing LGBTQ+-inclusive invitations is not just about ticking boxes; it's about infusing your invitations with the love, diversity, and pride that define your relationship. Every detail, from language choices to color palettes, becomes an opportunity to celebrate the beauty of LGBTQ+ love and to extend a warm and inclusive invitation to every guest. As you embark on this design journey, may your invitations become not just pieces of paper but heartfelt expressions of the love that binds you and the diverse community that surrounds and celebrates your union.

Managing Guest Lists and RSVPs

The art of managing guest lists and RSVPs is a delicate dance of logistics, consideration, and a sprinkle of excitement. This section guides you through the intricacies of creating a guest list that aligns with your vision while navigating the RSVP process with grace and ease.

Begin the journey by envisioning the atmosphere you desire for your celebration. Are you dreaming of an intimate gathering with your closest friends and family, or is your vision a grand affair filled with laughter and joy from a larger circle of loved ones? Your guest list sets the stage for the energy and vibe of your wedding day, so take a moment to visualize the faces that will surround you as you say your vows.

Create a preliminary guest list with your partner, considering immediate family, close friends, and any additional circles you wish to include. Be mindful of venue capacity, budget constraints, and any specific preferences you both have. Remember, this is a collaborative effort, and compromise may be necessary to strike the right balance.

Communication is key in managing guest lists. Keep an open dialogue with family members, especially if there are expectations or cultural considerations that may influence your choices. Transparency about your vision for an intimate gathering or a larger celebration can help manage expectations and foster understanding.

As you finalize your guest list, consider the potential for unexpected guests or last-minute additions. While it's important to stay within your venue's capacity, having a bit of flexibility in your numbers can alleviate stress if unforeseen circumstances arise. Communicate with your venue to understand their policies and any flexibility they may offer.

Once your guest list is in place, it's time to embark on the RSVP journey. Choose a method that aligns with your preferences, whether it's traditional paper RSVP cards, online forms, or a combination of both. Ensure that your RSVP deadline allows enough time for you to finalize details with your vendors and make any necessary adjustments to the seating plan.

Navigating RSVPs can be both exciting and challenging. Be prepared for a mix of enthusiastic responses, thoughtful regrets, and a few stragglers who may require gentle reminders. Keep track of responses in an organized manner, noting any dietary restrictions or special requests to ensure that every guest feels seen and accommodated.

Be prepared to handle unexpected changes. Life is dynamic, and unforeseen circumstances may arise that affect your guest list. Whether it's last-minute additions, changes in attendance, or unforeseen challenges, approach these changes with flexibility and grace. Keeping a positive and adaptable mindset ensures that you can navigate any surprises with ease.

Consider creating a designated point of contact for guests to reach out with questions or concerns. This could be a designated email address or phone number specifically for wedding-related inquiries. Having a streamlined communication channel helps manage queries efficiently and ensures that everyone is on the same page.

As you manage guest lists and RSVPs, remember that this process is not just about numbers; it's about curating a gathering of individuals who will share in the joy of your union. Every name on your list is a chapter in the story of your love, and every RSVP is a warm acknowledgment of the shared celebration that awaits. So, embrace the process, communicate openly, and let the journey of managing guest lists and RSVPs be a joyful step towards the beautiful tapestry of your wedding day.

Navigating Potential Etiquette Challenges

As you embark on the journey of wedding planning, navigating potential etiquette challenges is part and parcel of the process. From managing delicate family dynamics to addressing unexpected situations, this section offers guidance on approaching these challenges with grace and consideration.

One of the most common etiquette challenges revolves around the delicate dance of family dynamics. Whether it's divorced parents, blended families, or other complex relationships, crafting a guest list that honors everyone's feelings requires finesse. Consider having open and honest conversations with family members to understand their preferences and sensitivities. While it may not be possible to accommodate every request, demonstrating a willingness to listen and find compromises can go a long way in fostering understanding.

The plus-one dilemma is another area that often requires careful navigation. Determining who receives a plus-one invitation can be influenced by factors like the size of your venue, budget constraints, and the overall tone of your celebration. Be clear and consistent in your approach—whether it's extending plus-ones to all guests in established relationships or limiting them to those who are married or engaged. Communicate your decision tactfully on your invitations or wedding website to set clear expectations.

Invitations can be a potential minefield of etiquette challenges, especially when it comes to addressing them. Traditional etiquette dictates certain rules, but modern celebrations often call for more flexible approaches. If navigating the intricacies of addressing envelopes feels like walking on eggshells, consider consulting with a wedding etiquette expert or using online resources to guide you through the process. Remember, the goal is to convey warmth and respect in a way that aligns with your style.

The question of children at weddings is another etiquette challenge that couples often grapple with. While some couples embrace the idea of a family-friendly celebration, others may prefer a more adult-oriented atmosphere. Be clear and consistent in communicating your stance on children attending the wedding. You can achieve this through polite phrasing on invitations or creating a separate space or childcare options for families who may prefer an adult-only event.

The delicate matter of declining invitations is an aspect that requires both empathy and understanding. Guests may decline for various reasons, ranging from personal commitments to health concerns. Respond graciously to declines, expressing understanding and appreciation for their consideration. Avoid pressing for details, as some guests may prefer to keep the reasons for their absence private.

Handling last-minute RSVP changes can be a stress-inducing challenge, but approaching it with flexibility is key. Life is unpredictable, and unforeseen circumstances may arise that affect attendance. Whether it's unexpected additions or changes in plans, maintain a positive mindset and adjust accordingly. Having a buffer in your guest count can help accommodate these changes without causing undue stress.

Gift etiquette is an area that may require some thought, especially if you're contemplating a registry. While it's customary for guests to bring gifts, some may opt for alternative expressions of goodwill. Be appreciative of the sentiments behind every gift, whether it aligns with your registry or takes a more personalized form. Express gratitude promptly and sincerely.

Ultimately, the key to navigating potential etiquette challenges is open communication, empathy, and a willingness to find solutions that align with your vision while respecting the feelings and expectations of others. Approach these challenges with a sense of humor, remembering that every wedding is a unique blend of personalities, relationships, and unexpected moments. As you navigate the twists and turns of etiquette challenges, may your journey be filled with understanding, joy, and the knowledge that, at the heart of it all, your celebration is a testament to the love that binds you and the community that surrounds you.

Entertainment and Music

Step into the spotlight as we venture into the heart of Chapter 7: Entertainment and Music—an exploration of the sonic landscape that will set the rhythm for your wedding celebration. In this chapter, we dive into the world of entertainment, where every beat, melody, and moment contributes to the symphony of joy that defines your special day.

Entertainment is the heartbeat of any celebration, and your wedding day is no exception. Whether you're dreaming of a dance floor that pulsates with energy or an intimate gathering infused with soulful tunes, the choices you make in this chapter will create the soundtrack to your love story.

Music, like love, transcends boundaries, and this chapter is your guide to curating a playlist that mirrors the heartbeat of your relationship. From the ceremony to the reception, every note is an opportunity to share the melodies that resonate with your journey. We'll explore the art of selecting songs that capture the essence of your love, whether it's a timeless classic, a contemporary favorite, or a hidden gem that holds a special place in your hearts.

But the world of entertainment extends beyond music alone. This chapter also delves into the diverse realm of wedding entertainment options. Whether you envision a live band that elevates the energy, a

DJ who spins the tracks that define your love story, or even unique performances that add a touch of theatricality to your celebration, the choices are as limitless as your imagination.

Consider the atmosphere you wish to create—whether it's a lively celebration that has everyone on their feet or a more subdued ambiance that encourages intimate conversations. The entertainment you choose becomes the conductor of the emotional symphony, guiding your guests through a journey of laughter, joy, and perhaps a few happy tears.

As you navigate the myriad options in entertainment and music, remember that this chapter is an invitation to infuse your celebration with the beats that define your love. Your choices in this realm are more than just tunes and performances; they are the orchestrators of memories, the creators of moments, and the architects of an experience that will linger in the hearts of your guests long after the last dance.

So, as you step into Chapter 8, may the melodies you choose be a reflection of your love's unique rhythm. May the entertainment you select amplify the joy, laughter, and celebration that define your union. And may this chapter guide you in curating an experience that not only resonates with your love story but also ensures that every guest leaves the dance floor with a heart full of cherished memories.

Selecting LGBTQ+ Friendly DJs and Bands

In the rich tapestry of wedding planning, one of the most vibrant threads is the music that will echo through the celebration. As you curate the soundtrack to your special day, an essential consideration is selecting LGBTQ+ friendly DJs and bands—musical maestros who not only understand the diverse tastes of your guests but also embrace and celebrate the beautiful spectrum of love.

The significance of choosing LGBTQ+ friendly DJs and bands goes beyond their ability to mix beats or perform live. It's about creating an atmosphere of acceptance, understanding, and celebration that resonates with the unique love stories of every couple. Whether you're envisioning a dance floor that pulses with the energy of a thousand beats or a more laid-back celebration infused with soulful melodies, finding musical partners who align with your vision is paramount.

Begin your search by seeking out DJs and bands with a reputation for inclusivity. In today's interconnected world, social media and online platforms provide valuable insights into the ethos and values of potential musical partners. Look for performers who not only showcase their musical talents but also express a commitment to creating a welcoming space for diverse audiences.

Engage in open and transparent conversations with prospective DJs and bands. A LGBTQ+ friendly performer is not just someone who plays a great set; they are allies who understand the importance of curating a playlist that reflects the diversity of love. Discuss your vision, share your favorite genres, and explore how they approach inclusivity in their performances. This dialogue not only ensures that your musical tastes align but also sets the foundation for an inclusive celebration.

Consider the repertoire of the DJs or bands you're considering. A LGBTQ+ friendly DJ or band should be well-versed in a broad range of music that appeals to diverse audiences. Whether it's classic hits, contemporary chart-toppers, or anthems that hold special significance in the LGBTQ+ community, a versatile musical selection ensures that every guest finds a rhythm that resonates with them.

Explore testimonials and reviews from other couples who have collaborated with the DJs or bands on your radar. Pay attention not only to their musical prowess but also to the experiences of diverse couples who have celebrated their love with these performers. A track record of positive experiences is a promising sign that your chosen musical partners are adept at creating an inclusive and memorable celebration.

Inquire about their approach to pronouns and announcements during the event. A LGBTQ+ friendly DJ or band will understand the importance of using inclusive language that respects the identities of all couples. Discuss any specific preferences you have regarding announcements or introductions to ensure that your celebration reflects the nuances of your love story.

Lastly, trust your instincts. When it comes to selecting LGBTQ+ friendly DJs and bands, the connection goes beyond musical compatibility. It's about finding performers who not only play the right notes but also resonate with the heartbeat of your love. If you feel a genuine connection with a DJ or band, if their passion aligns with your vision, and if their commitment to inclusivity shines through, you've likely found the perfect musical partners for your celebration.

In the realm of wedding music, LGBTQ+ friendly DJs and bands are not just performers; they are collaborators in the symphony of your love story. As you embark on this journey of selecting the musical architects of your celebration, may you find partners who not only play the tunes that make your hearts dance but also contribute to the harmonious celebration of love in all its beautiful forms.

Creating a Diverse and Inclusive Playlist

The heartbeat of your wedding celebration is the playlist—a carefully curated collection of songs that tell the story of your love, stir emotions, and beckon guests to the dance floor. When it comes to crafting a playlist that resonates with the diverse tapestry of your love and community, the key lies in creating a diverse and inclusive musical journey.

Music has a universal language that transcends boundaries, and your wedding playlist is an opportunity to celebrate this diversity. Start by reflecting on the musical genres and artists that hold special significance for both you and your partner. Whether it's the soulful ballads that define your love story, the anthems that have been the soundtrack to your journey, or the beats that make you want to dance, these personal touches infuse the playlist with authenticity.

Consider the wide range of tastes among your guests. A diverse and inclusive playlist caters to the varied musical preferences of your loved ones. While your favorites are undoubtedly central to the selection, incorporating a mix of genres—from pop to rock, R&B to country, and everything in between—ensures that every guest finds a melody that resonates with them. This inclusivity makes the dance floor a space where everyone feels invited to celebrate.

Explore the rich world of LGBTQ+ anthems and artists. The LGBTQ+ community has a vibrant musical history with anthems that hold deep meaning for many. Incorporating these tunes into your playlist not only pays homage to this rich tradition but also creates moments of connection and celebration for members of the community. From classics like "I Will Survive" to contemporary hits that celebrate love in all its forms, these songs add layers of significance to your celebration.

Infuse cultural diversity into your playlist. If you and your partner come from different cultural backgrounds, consider including songs that reflect these roots. Whether it's a traditional folk tune, a classic from your cultural heritage, or a modern fusion track that represents the blend of your identities, these selections add a layer of richness to the playlist. It's an opportunity to share and celebrate the diverse backgrounds that make your union unique.

Be mindful of the lyrics and messages conveyed in the songs. While upbeat tunes are essential for a lively celebration, pay attention to the lyrics to ensure that they align with the inclusive and celebratory atmosphere you want to create. Consider songs that promote love, unity, and joy, steering clear of any that may convey messages inconsistent with the values of your celebration.

Collaborate with your DJ or band to understand their approach to inclusivity. A professional DJ or band with experience in LGBTQ+ friendly events will have insights into creating a playlist that embraces diversity. Share your vision, discuss specific songs or genres that are meaningful to you, and explore how they can weave these elements into the overall musical journey of your celebration.

Remember that creating a diverse and inclusive playlist is not just about ticking boxes; it's about curating an experience that mirrors the spectrum of your love and the community that surrounds you. Each song becomes a note in the symphony of your celebration, contributing to the unique melody that defines your wedding day. As you embark on this musical journey, may your playlist be a harmonious blend of love, diversity, and the joyful celebration of your union.

Planning Entertainment for All Ages

In the joyful tapestry of a wedding celebration, ensuring entertainment that resonates with guests of all ages is akin to weaving a thread that connects generations. From the littlest flower girl to the seasoned dance floor enthusiasts, planning entertainment that spans the age spectrum contributes to an inclusive and memorable celebration for everyone present.

Begin by envisioning the atmosphere you want to create. Your wedding day is a blend of moments—from the heartfelt ceremony to the lively reception—and each phase presents opportunities to engage guests of all ages. Consider the diverse tastes and preferences within your guest list, and strive to strike a balance that keeps everyone entertained and involved.

During the ceremony, aim for a blend of traditional and modern elements that resonate with different age groups. While timeless classical pieces create an elegant and solemn ambiance, consider incorporating contemporary tunes that hold significance for you and your partner. This fusion of old and new ensures that everyone feels connected to the emotional journey of the ceremony.

When it comes to the reception, the dance floor becomes a stage for intergenerational celebration. Your playlist, as discussed in the previous section, plays a crucial role in creating an atmosphere that encourages guests of all ages to join the festivities. From the latest chart-toppers to classic hits that evoke nostalgia, the diverse musical journey should be a tapestry that caters to a broad range of tastes.

Consider interactive elements that engage both young and old. Photo booths, where guests can capture moments of joy, are a hit across generations. Include props that add a touch of whimsy and creativity, encouraging guests of all ages to unleash their playful side. Interactive games like lawn games or trivia can also be enjoyed by guests of various ages, fostering a sense of camaraderie.

Create a designated space for the little ones. If your guest list includes children, providing entertainment tailored to their age group ensures that they have a delightful experience. Consider hiring a children's entertainer, setting up a craft corner, or having a dedicated area with games and activities. This thoughtful inclusion allows parents to enjoy the celebration while ensuring that the youngest guests are entertained and engaged.

Explore entertainment options beyond the dance floor. While dancing is a universal form of celebration, not everyone may be eager to showcase their moves. Incorporate alternative entertainment options, such as live performers, acrobats, or even a themed performance that adds a layer of excitement to the celebration. This eclectic mix ensures that every guest finds a form of entertainment that resonates with their preferences.

Engage with your entertainment providers to understand their ability to cater to diverse audiences. DJs or bands experienced in weddings will have insights into creating a setlist that appeals to various age groups. Discuss the possibility of incorporating special moments or dedications that acknowledge different generations, creating a sense of connection and inclusivity.

Lastly, encourage cross-generational interactions. Whether it's through a heartfelt speech that transcends generations or a dance-off that spans ages, fostering moments where guests of different ages come together creates a sense of unity. These shared experiences become cherished memories that reflect the spirit of your celebration.

In planning entertainment for all ages, remember that your wedding day is a tapestry that weaves together the stories and experiences of everyone present. From the laughter of children to the dance moves of grandparents, each moment contributes to the beautiful mosaic of your celebration. As you navigate the intricacies of planning entertainment, may your choices create a space where every guest, regardless of age, feels embraced, entertained, and a vital part of the joyful symphony of your wedding day.

Culinary Experiences

As we enter the delectable realm of Chapter 8, our journey unfolds into the culinary tapestry that will tantalize your taste buds and elevate your wedding celebration to a feast of flavors. Welcome to a chapter dedicated to the art of gastronomy, where every bite becomes a celebration of love, culture, and the joy of shared meals.

In the intricate dance of wedding planning, the culinary experiences you curate for your guests are more than just a meal—they are a celebration of love through the language of food. From the first bite that graces the palate to the sweet notes of dessert that linger, each dish becomes a chapter in the story of your union, creating a sensory experience that echoes the uniqueness of your love.

This chapter is your guide to navigating the world of wedding cuisine, from selecting a menu that reflects your tastes to infusing cultural influences that add depth to the dining experience. Whether you envision an elegant plated affair, a bountiful buffet, or a fusion of culinary styles that mirrors the diversity of your love, the choices you make in this chapter will leave an indelible mark on your wedding day.

We'll explore the nuances of menu planning, considering dietary preferences, cultural influences, and the seasonality of ingredients. From the appetizers that spark conversation to the main course that becomes a culinary symphony, this chapter delves into the art of creating a menu that not only satisfies the appetite but also tells a story.

Beyond the plates and platters, we'll also unravel the elements that elevate the dining experience. The ambience, the presentation, and the service—all contribute to the overall culinary journey of your celebration. Whether you're dreaming of an intimate family-style dinner or a grand feast that mirrors a banquet, this chapter guides you in orchestrating a dining experience that aligns with your vision.

So, as we embark on the exploration of culinary experiences, may your taste buds dance with delight, may your guests savor every moment, and may the dining table become a place where the love you share is savored in every bite. Get ready to savor the flavors of love as we dive into the delectable journey that is Chapter 9: Culinary Experiences.

Exploring LGBTQ+-Friendly Catering Options

In the symphony of wedding planning, the culinary notes you choose play a pivotal role in creating an unforgettable experience for you and your guests. As you embark on the journey of selecting catering options, exploring LGBTQ+-friendly choices is a delightful step toward crafting a celebration that reflects inclusivity, understanding, and the celebration of diverse love stories.

When seeking LGBTQ+-friendly catering options, think beyond the menu and consider the values and inclusivity practices of potential caterers. A LGBTQ+-friendly caterer is not just someone who prepares delicious dishes; they are allies who understand and embrace the beautiful spectrum of love that defines your celebration.

Begin by researching catering companies with a reputation for inclusivity. In today's interconnected world, online reviews, testimonials, and social media platforms provide valuable insights into the ethos of potential catering partners. Look for caterers who not only showcase their culinary expertise but also express a commitment to creating a welcoming space for diverse couples and celebrations.

Engage in open and transparent conversations with potential caterers. A LGBTQ+-friendly caterer is someone who not only caters to your culinary preferences but also understands the importance of fostering an environment where every guest feels celebrated and respected. Discuss your vision for the celebration, any specific cultural influences you'd like to incorporate into the menu, and how they approach inclusivity in their services.

Consider the flexibility and creativity of catering options. LGBTQ+-friendly caterers often exhibit a willingness to adapt and customize their offerings to align with the unique preferences and cultural influences of each couple. Whether you have specific dietary considerations, cultural traditions you'd like to incorporate, or a vision for a diverse and inclusive menu, a caterer who embraces these aspects enhances the personalization of your culinary experience.

Explore LGBTQ+ affirming partnerships. Some catering companies actively seek partnerships with LGBTQ+ organizations or events, demonstrating a commitment to supporting and celebrating the community. Inquiring about any LGBTQ+ affirming collaborations or initiatives can provide additional insights into a caterer's dedication to inclusivity beyond their culinary offerings.

Taste testing is an essential step in the process. Arrange for tastings with potential caterers to not only experience the flavors of their dishes but also to assess their willingness to accommodate your preferences. A caterer who values your input, embraces your culinary vision, and ensures that your menu reflects the diversity of your celebration is a valuable partner in creating a memorable dining experience.

Consider the presentation and service elements. The overall dining experience extends beyond the taste of the food. Assess how potential caterers approach presentation, table settings, and service. A LGBTQ+-friendly caterer is attuned to the importance of creating an inclusive and welcoming atmosphere for all guests, ensuring that the dining experience is a harmonious and enjoyable part of the celebration.

As you explore LGBTQ+-friendly catering options, remember that your wedding menu is more than just a collection of dishes—it's a reflection of your love story and the community you've gathered to celebrate with. Each bite becomes a symbol of inclusivity, understanding, and the joy that comes from sharing a meal in the company of loved ones. So, as you embark on this culinary exploration, may you find a catering partner who not only satisfies your taste buds but also celebrates the beautiful tapestry of love that defines your wedding celebration.

Designing a Menu that Reflects Your Relationship

In the culinary canvas of your wedding celebration, the menu becomes a vibrant brushstroke, painting a picture that is uniquely yours. As you embark on the exciting journey of designing a menu, the opportunity arises to weave the flavors, textures, and cultural influences that define your relationship into a gastronomic tapestry that mirrors the essence of your love story.

Start by reflecting on the culinary experiences that hold significance for both you and your partner. The shared meals, the favorite dishes, and the cultural influences that have shaped your palate—all become ingredients in the recipe of your wedding menu. Consider the flavors that evoke cherished memories, the aromas that transport you to special moments, and the dishes that symbolize the journey of your love.

Think beyond traditional boundaries and infuse your menu with personal touches. Your wedding day is a celebration of your unique love story, and the menu is an opportunity to showcase your individuality. Whether it's incorporating elements from your cultural backgrounds, infusing flavors that represent pivotal moments in your relationship, or featuring dishes that hold sentimental value, each choice becomes a chapter in the culinary narrative of your celebration.

Consider your favorite cuisines and explore creative ways to integrate them into the menu. Whether you share a love for Italian pasta, Japanese sushi, or Mexican tacos, incorporating elements from your favorite cuisines adds a layer of personalization to the dining experience. Collaborate with your caterer to design a menu that showcases a variety of flavors and dishes that resonate with both of you.

Reflect on your journey as a couple and consider thematic elements for the menu. If your love story has traversed different cities or countries, a menu inspired by the places that hold significance can be a delightful touch. Each dish becomes a chapter in your journey, allowing guests to taste the flavors of the locations that have played a role in your relationship.

Consider dietary preferences and restrictions to ensure inclusivity. As you design a menu that reflects your relationship, take into account the diverse dietary needs of your guests. Whether it's vegetarian, vegan, gluten-free, or other considerations, offering a variety of options ensures that every guest can partake in the culinary celebration.

Collaborate closely with your caterer to bring your vision to life. A skilled caterer not only prepares delicious dishes but also serves as a culinary collaborator, translating your vision into a menu that delights the senses. Share your inspirations, preferences, and any specific cultural or thematic elements you'd like to incorporate. The more you engage with your caterer, the more personalized and reflective of your relationship your menu will become.

Consider unique and interactive dining experiences. Elevate your culinary journey by exploring unique dining concepts or interactive food stations. Whether it's a live cooking demonstration, a custom cocktail bar, or a dessert station that encourages guests to create their own sweet treats, these elements add an engaging and memorable touch to the dining experience.

Remember, your wedding menu is more than just a collection of dishes; it's a culinary love letter that tells the story of your relationship. With each bite, your guests embark on a journey through the flavors, cultures, and shared moments that define your love story. As you design a menu that reflects your relationship, may the dining experience become a cherished part of your wedding celebration, inviting everyone to savor the unique and delicious tale of your union.

Accommodating Dietary Restrictions and Preferences

In the diverse landscape of wedding celebrations, one of the key considerations when designing your menu is accommodating the varied dietary restrictions and preferences of your guests. The art of hospitality extends beyond creating a sumptuous spread—it lies in ensuring that every guest, regardless of their dietary needs, can partake in the culinary celebration. As you navigate this aspect of menu planning, consider it an opportunity to create an inclusive and delightful dining experience for all.

Start by gathering information on dietary restrictions from your guests. In the invitation or RSVP process, provide an opportunity for guests to communicate any dietary restrictions or preferences they may have. This initial step allows you to be proactive in addressing specific needs, ensuring that everyone feels considered and valued in the culinary journey of your celebration.

Engage in open communication with your caterer regarding dietary considerations. A skilled and experienced caterer understands the importance of creating a menu that accommodates a range of dietary needs. Share the information collected from your guests, and collaborate with your caterer to design a menu that offers diverse options, ensuring that everyone can partake in the joyous feast.

Consider the broad spectrum of dietary preferences. In today's world, dietary preferences encompass a wide range, from vegetarian and vegan to gluten-free, dairy-free, and more. Designing a menu that includes options for various dietary preferences ensures that every guest has the opportunity to savor the flavors of your celebration. A diverse and inclusive menu caters to the culinary tastes of all, making the dining experience a shared celebration.

Explore creative and flavorful alternatives for specific dietary needs. A misconception about accommodating dietary restrictions is that it involves sacrificing flavor or variety. On the contrary, this is an opportunity to discover innovative and delicious alternatives. Collaborate with your caterer to explore plant-based delights, gluten-free grains, dairy-free delights, and other creative options that add depth and diversity to the menu.

Ensure clear labeling and communication of dietary information. When presenting the menu to your guests, whether on printed materials or through waitstaff, ensure clear and comprehensive labeling of dishes, indicating which ones are suitable for specific dietary restrictions. Transparent communication helps guests navigate the options with ease, ensuring that they make choices aligned with their needs.

Consider cross-contamination prevention, especially for severe allergies. If certain guests have severe allergies, discuss with your caterer the measures in place to prevent cross-contamination in the kitchen. An experienced caterer will have protocols to safeguard against allergen cross-contact, ensuring the safety of guests with allergies.

Be attentive to cultural and religious dietary practices. In addition to individual dietary restrictions, consider any cultural or religious dietary practices that may be present among your guests. If you are aware of specific customs or requirements, communicate these details to your caterer to ensure that the menu aligns with the diverse cultural and religious backgrounds of your guests.

Remember that dietary accommodation is a gesture of hospitality and inclusivity. By thoughtfully designing a menu that caters to a variety of dietary needs, you create a dining experience where every guest feels seen, respected, and able to fully participate in the culinary celebration of your wedding day. Embracing diversity in the menu not only ensures that everyone can enjoy the feast but also reflects the spirit of inclusivity that defines your celebration. As you navigate this aspect of menu planning, may your choices contribute to a dining experience that is as diverse and rich as the love you're celebrating.

Capturing Memories

In the kaleidoscope of your wedding day, moments unfold like petals, each one unique and fleeting. As we delve into Chapter 9, we embark on the journey of capturing memories—a chapter that transcends the immediate celebration, weaving the tapestry of your love story into tangible snapshots that will be cherished for a lifetime. Welcome to a realm where every smile, every glance, and every embrace becomes a brushstroke in the masterpiece of your wedding memories.

Photography and videography are the storytellers of your wedding day. They freeze time, preserving the laughter, the tears, and the moments that define the essence of your union. This chapter is a guide to navigating the world of capturing memories, from selecting the right professionals to ensuring that every nuance of your celebration is immortalized in visual tales that will transport you back to the magic of your wedding day.

As you step into this chapter, consider it a voyage into the art of storytelling through imagery. Each photograph, each frame of the video, is a chapter in the narrative of your love. The seasoned professionals behind the lens are not mere photographers and videographers; they are the custodians of your memories, entrusted with the task of encapsulating the emotion, the beauty, and the fleeting instants that make your wedding day extraordinary.

We'll explore the intricacies of choosing the right photography and videography style that aligns with your vision. From the candid shots that capture the spontaneous joy to the posed portraits that showcase the elegance of your union, the choices you make in this chapter shape the visual narrative of your love story.

Consider the role of technology and innovation in modern wedding storytelling. Drones, 360-degree cameras, and other cutting-edge technologies have opened new horizons in capturing memories. We'll delve into how these tools can add a dynamic and immersive dimension to your wedding documentation, creating a visual legacy that goes beyond the conventional.

This chapter also guides you in preparing for the photography and videography sessions. From creating a shot list that ensures no moment is overlooked to collaborating with your chosen professionals to articulate your vision, the preparation phase is a crucial element in the storytelling process.

Remember that the magic lies not just in the grand moments but in the subtleties—the stolen glances, the heartfelt exchanges, and the tender gestures that define the unique alchemy of your relationship. The professionals you choose for this task are not mere observers; they are your visual poets, translating the language of love into a timeless narrative.

So, as we delve into the art of capturing memories, may your wedding day be immortalized in images and videos that not only reflect the beauty of the celebration but also evoke the emotions, the connections, and the essence of your love. Get ready to embark on a visual journey through Chapter 10, where every frame is a page in the story of your extraordinary love.

Hiring LGBTQ+-Friendly Photographers and Videographers

In the vibrant mosaic of wedding planning, one of the pivotal decisions you'll make is selecting the storytellers who will capture the visual narrative of your celebration. Photographers and videographers are not just professionals behind the lens; they are the artists entrusted with translating the emotions, the moments, and the essence of your love story into tangible memories. As we delve into the intricacies of hiring LGBTQ+-friendly photographers and videographers, it's essential to recognize that the lens through which your story is told holds the power to shape the narrative and reflect the inclusivity of your celebration.

Start your search by seeking professionals with a reputation for inclusivity. In the contemporary landscape of wedding photography and videography, many professionals actively embrace and celebrate diversity. This goes beyond a portfolio—it's about finding individuals who resonate with the richness of love in all its forms and who have demonstrated their commitment to inclusivity through their work and collaborations.

Explore the portfolios and past projects of potential photographers and videographers. The visual storytelling of LGBTQ+ weddings requires an understanding of the nuances, emotions, and cultural elements that define these celebrations. As you peruse their portfolios, look for diverse representations that showcase a range of love stories, capturing the unique essence of each couple. This not only demonstrates technical proficiency but also a genuine appreciation for the diversity of love.

Engage in open and transparent communication during the selection process. The professionals you choose are not just there to document your wedding day; they are partners in the creation of your visual legacy. During initial consultations, ask questions about their approach to LGBTQ+ weddings, their understanding of diverse love stories, and how they ensure that every couple feels seen and celebrated through their work.

Consider the importance of a pre-wedding connection. Building rapport with your chosen photographers and videographers contributes to a more authentic and comfortable documentation of your celebration. Look for professionals who are not just skilled in their craft but also prioritize establishing a connection with their clients, ensuring that the trust and comfort necessary for capturing intimate moments are present.

Discuss your vision for the visual narrative of your wedding. Each couple's love story is unique, and your chosen photographers and videographers should be attuned to the elements that make yours extraordinary. Share your vision, discuss any specific cultural or thematic elements you'd like to incorporate, and ensure that your chosen professionals are enthusiastic about translating your ideas into visual poetry.

Review contracts and policies to ensure LGBTQ+ inclusivity. A LGBTQ+-friendly photographer or videographer is not just about talent—it's also about the policies and values of the professional you choose. Review contracts and terms to ensure that they align with an inclusive approach, guaranteeing that you and your partner feel supported and respected throughout the entire process.

Seek recommendations from the LGBTQ+ community. Word of mouth is a powerful tool in the wedding industry. Reach out to the LGBTQ+ community for recommendations and testimonials about photographers and videographers who have not only demonstrated technical expertise but have also created an inclusive and affirming experience for couples.

Remember, the photographers and videographers you choose are more than documentarians; they are visual poets who craft the narrative of your love story. By intentionally selecting LGBTQ+-friendly professionals, you are ensuring that your celebration is captured through a lens that not only appreciates but actively celebrates the diverse spectrum of love. As you embark on this journey, may your chosen storytellers become partners in crafting a visual legacy that reflects the beauty, the joy, and the inclusivity of your extraordinary love story.

Creating a Shot List and Capturing Candid Moments

As you step into the realm of capturing memories, one of the key aspects of orchestrating your visual narrative is crafting a shot list that strikes a balance between planned moments and candid spontaneity.

Creating a shot list is like sketching the framework of your visual story —it provides guidance to your photographers and videographers while leaving room for the magic that unfolds naturally. In this section, we explore the art of balancing a structured shot list with the beauty of capturing candid moments, ensuring that every facet of your celebration is immortalized in a visual tapestry that is uniquely yours.

Begin by envisioning the story you want your visual narrative to tell. What are the key moments, emotions, and interactions that hold special significance? Your shot list is a reflection of your vision, serving as a roadmap for your photographers and videographers to navigate the essential elements of your celebration. Consider the milestones, the rituals, and the details that are important to you, ensuring that they find a place in your curated list.

Engage in open communication with your chosen professionals. Once you've drafted your initial shot list, share it with your photographers and videographers during pre-wedding consultations. This collaborative approach allows for a dialogue where you can articulate the vision behind each shot, discuss any cultural or thematic elements you'd like to incorporate, and ensure that your chosen professionals are aligned with your expectations.

Consider the importance of candid moments in your shot list. While planned shots capture the essence of specific moments, candid moments infuse your visual story with authenticity and emotion. Discuss with your photographers and videographers the significance of capturing spontaneous interactions, emotions, and expressions. A skillful professional knows how to blend into the background, allowing these moments to unfold organically.

Strike a balance between formal and informal shots. Your shot list should encompass a mix of formal portraits and informal, candid shots. Formal shots capture the elegance and poise of your celebration, showcasing the beauty of posed moments. On the other hand, candid shots breathe life into your visual narrative, preserving the unscripted joy, laughter, and connection that make your celebration uniquely yours.

Trust in the expertise of your chosen professionals. While a shot list is a valuable guide, it's essential to trust in the creative expertise of your photographers and videographers. These professionals bring a wealth of experience and an artistic eye to your celebration. Allow them the freedom to capture spontaneous moments, explore unique angles, and infuse their creativity into the visual tapestry of your wedding day.

Be flexible and open to serendipity. Some of the most cherished moments in a visual narrative are the unexpected and unplanned ones. Be open to the serendipity of the day, allowing your photographers and videographers the freedom to seize unique moments as they unfold. These unscripted gems often become the heartbeats of your visual story, encapsulating the genuine spirit of your celebration.

Review and adjust your shot list as needed. In the dynamic landscape of wedding celebrations, plans may evolve, and moments may unfold differently than anticipated. Periodically review and adjust your shot list as needed, ensuring that it remains reflective of your vision while allowing for the flexibility required to capture the organic beauty of your celebration.

Creating a shot list and capturing candid moments is a delicate dance between structure and spontaneity. It's a choreography where planned poses harmonize with unscripted laughter, and where every frame tells a story of love, connection, and celebration. As you embark on this aspect of capturing memories, may your shot list be a guiding star, and may the candid moments become the soulful melodies that resonate through the visual symphony of your wedding day.

Preserving Memories for a Lifetime

As your wedding day unfolds and the moments are immortalized through the lens, the culmination of these visual treasures becomes the foundation of your cherished memories. In this section, we explore the art of preserving memories for a lifetime—a journey that extends beyond the day itself, transforming your celebration into a timeless legacy that you and future generations can revisit with joy and nostalgia.

Invest in high-quality prints and albums to bring your memories to life. While digital files are convenient for sharing and storing, there's an unparalleled charm in holding tangible prints and flipping through beautifully crafted albums. Invest in high-quality prints that capture the vibrancy and emotion of each moment. A thoughtfully designed album becomes a narrative, allowing you to relive the chapters of your wedding day in a tangible and immersive way.

Consider the role of technology in preserving and sharing memories. Digital advancements have introduced innovative ways to preserve and share your wedding memories. Explore options such as online galleries, cloud storage, and personalized websites that not only serve as secure archives but also provide a convenient means of sharing your visual story with friends and family, regardless of geographical distances.

Create a designated space for your visual legacy. Whether it's a gallery wall in your home, a dedicated photo bookshelf, or a personalized display in a digital frame, carve out a space that honors your visual legacy. Select key moments, highlight your favorite shots, and curate a display that serves as a constant reminder of the love, joy, and beauty that defined your wedding day.

Engage in storytelling through videography. While photographs freeze moments in time, videography adds a dynamic and immersive dimension to your visual narrative. Your wedding video is a moving tapestry of emotions, capturing not just the still frames but the cadence of laughter, the exchange of vows, and the rhythm of your celebration. Invest in professional videography to ensure that your memories are preserved with the same care and artistry as your photographs.

Share your memories with loved ones. Your wedding memories are not just for you; they are a shared celebration with friends and family who witnessed and contributed to the magic of your day. Host viewing sessions, create personalized photo books as gifts, and share snippets of your video on social media. By extending the joy of your memories, you invite others to partake in the love that surrounded your celebration.

Preserve the raw and unedited moments. While polished and edited shots have their place, don't underestimate the power of preserving the raw and unedited moments. Consider creating a collection of untouched and unfiltered shots that capture the authenticity and spontaneity of your celebration. These unaltered glimpses become precious time capsules, transporting you back to the genuine emotions of your wedding day.

Consider the future and generational impact of your visual legacy. Your wedding memories have the potential to transcend generations, becoming a precious inheritance for those who come after you. When preserving your memories, consider the long-term impact and how future generations can access and appreciate the visual legacy of your love story. Invest in archival-quality prints and storage solutions that ensure the longevity of your treasured memories.

Embrace the beauty of imperfection and authenticity. In the quest for perfect shots, remember that the true beauty of your memories lies in their imperfection and authenticity. The unscripted laughter, the candid moments, and the spontaneous expressions—these are the elements that make your visual narrative uniquely yours. Embrace the imperfections, for they are the brushstrokes that add character to the canvas of your memories.

As you embark on the journey of preserving memories for a lifetime, may each photograph, each print, and each frame of your wedding video become a timeless capsule of love. May your visual legacy not only tell the story of your celebration but also evoke the emotions, the connections, and the enduring beauty of the extraordinary love you shared on your wedding day.

CHAPTER 10

Inclusivity: A Focus on Trans Men

In the ever-evolving tapestry of love and celebration, we arrive at a chapter that places a spotlight on a vital aspect of inclusivity—welcoming and honoring the experiences of trans men in the realm of wedding planning. Every love story is unique, and this chapter is dedicated to ensuring that the journey of wedding planning resonates with the diverse experiences and needs of trans men. In the spirit of celebration and unity, we embark on a thoughtful exploration of how to navigate the landscape of wedding planning with inclusivity at the forefront.

As we delve into the nuances of wedding planning for trans men, it's essential to recognize the diversity within the LGBTQ+ community. Trans men bring their unique perspectives, identities, and experiences to the celebration of love, and this chapter aims to provide insights, considerations, and supportive guidance tailored to their specific needs.

Throughout this chapter, we'll explore various facets of wedding planning through an inclusive lens, acknowledging the importance of representation, sensitivity, and understanding. From fashion choices that align with personal styles to considerations for inclusive ceremonies that honor diverse identities, the focus is on creating a space where every trans man can feel seen, celebrated, and empowered throughout the wedding planning journey.

Inclusivity is not just a concept but a commitment to embracing the rich tapestry of love in all its forms. As we embark on this chapter, may it serve as a guiding light, fostering a wedding planning experience that is affirming, respectful, and joyous for trans men and their partners. Together, let's explore the boundless possibilities of love and celebration, where every story is honored, every identity is celebrated, and every wedding is a testament to the beautifully diverse spectrum of human connection.

Recognizing the Unique Needs of Trans Men in Wedding Planning

In the beautifully diverse landscape of love, every individual's journey is uniquely their own, shaped by personal experiences, identities, and aspirations. As we delve into the realm of wedding planning, it becomes imperative to recognize and honor the specific needs and considerations of trans men. This section is a heartfelt exploration of how we can navigate the wedding planning journey with sensitivity, inclusivity, and a genuine understanding of the experiences that trans men bring to the celebration of love.

First and foremost, it's crucial to acknowledge that the needs of trans men in wedding planning are as varied as the individuals themselves. Each trans man has a distinct relationship with their gender identity, and their experiences may differ widely. It's essential to approach wedding planning with an open heart and a willingness to listen, ensuring that the celebration aligns with the unique preferences and desires of the trans man and their partner.

Fashion choices play a significant role in wedding planning, and for trans men, this aspect may involve considerations related to personal style, comfort, and gender expression. Recognizing the importance of inclusive attire options and providing a space for trans men to express their gender identity through fashion choices is a pivotal aspect of creating an affirming wedding planning experience.

Communication emerges as a cornerstone of navigating the unique needs of trans men. Open and respectful dialogues with trans individuals and their partners pave the way for understanding and accommodating specific preferences. Sensitivity to language, pronouns, and the use of inclusive terminology creates an environment where every voice is heard, and every identity is acknowledged with the utmost respect.

When selecting wedding vendors, including photographers, videographers, and planners, seeking professionals who are experienced in working with diverse couples is paramount. Professionals who understand the nuances of LGBTQ+ experiences, including those of trans individuals, bring a level of sensitivity and awareness that enriches the entire wedding planning process.

The choice of venue and ceremony also holds significance for trans men. Inclusive venues that understand and respect diverse identities contribute to creating a space where every individual feels affirmed. Similarly, crafting a ceremony that reflects the unique journey of the couple, including the experiences of a trans man, adds a personal touch to the celebration.

Furthermore, the emotional well-being of trans men during the wedding planning journey should not be overlooked. Navigating societal expectations, familial dynamics, and personal considerations can be complex. Providing support systems, whether through friends, family, or LGBTQ+-friendly resources, becomes instrumental in fostering a positive and empowering wedding planning experience.

In essence, recognizing the unique needs of trans men in wedding planning is a commitment to creating a celebration that authentically reflects their love story. It's about building a foundation of understanding, empathy, and respect, ensuring that every decision aligns with the couple's vision and affirms the identities of all individuals involved. As we venture into this exploration, may it serve as a guiding light for wedding planning experiences that honor the beautiful diversity of love, where every story is celebrated, and every identity is cherished.

Selecting Attire that Affirms Identity

In the kaleidoscope of wedding planning, the choice of attire holds profound significance. For trans men, this decision transcends the realms of style and fashion; it becomes a powerful means of expressing and affirming their gender identity on one of the most significant days of their lives. Navigating the landscape of wedding attire as a trans man involves considerations that go beyond conventional fashion choices, emphasizing the importance of inclusivity, comfort, and personal expression.

One of the key considerations for trans men in selecting wedding attire is the affirmation of their gender identity. Traditional gendered norms in wedding fashion may not fully encapsulate the diverse expressions of masculinity that trans men bring to the celebration. Recognizing this, the wedding industry has seen a positive shift towards more inclusive options, providing a range of styles that cater to various gender expressions.

Trans men may find empowerment in attire that aligns with their individual sense of masculinity. This could involve exploring suits or ensembles that reflect their personal style, whether that be a classic tailored suit, a more casual look, or even incorporating elements that hold cultural or sentimental significance. The journey of selecting attire becomes an opportunity for self-expression and authenticity.

Beyond aesthetics, the comfort of the chosen attire is paramount. Wedding celebrations often span several hours, encompassing various activities from the ceremony to the reception. Ensuring that the attire feels comfortable and allows for ease of movement is crucial for a positive and enjoyable experience. This may involve considerations such as the type of fabric, fit, and overall design.

Communication with fashion professionals plays a pivotal role in this process. Transparency and open dialogue with tailors, designers, and stylists are essential to ensure that the chosen attire aligns seamlessly with the trans man's vision and comfort level. Professionals experienced in working with diverse couples, including those with LGBTQ+

identities, can bring a heightened level of understanding and sensitivity to the fittings and customization process.

For some trans men, incorporating elements of personal or cultural significance into their attire may hold great importance. This could range from selecting colors that carry special meaning to integrating accessories that symbolize aspects of their journey. The process of selecting attire becomes a canvas upon which the unique narrative of the couple's love story is painted.

The support network surrounding the trans man in the wedding planning journey also plays a crucial role. Friends, family, and partners can provide invaluable encouragement and affirmation. Inclusivity within the support system ensures that the trans man feels seen, heard, and celebrated throughout the process of selecting attire—a process that goes beyond the superficial and taps into the core of identity.

In essence, selecting attire that affirms identity is an empowering and liberating aspect of wedding planning for trans men. It is a declaration of selfhood, a celebration of authenticity, and a moment of pride. As the wedding industry continues to embrace diversity, the choices available to trans men expand, providing a spectrum of options that align with the beautifully diverse expressions of masculinity. In this journey of self-expression through attire, may every trans man find the perfect ensemble that not only complements their style but also resonates with the authenticity of their identity on this momentous day of celebration.

Ensuring Inclusive Language and Representation

Language is a powerful tool that shapes our understanding of the world, and in the context of wedding planning, it becomes a vital aspect of creating an inclusive and affirming environment for trans men. This section delves into the importance of utilizing language that respects and acknowledges diverse gender identities, ensuring that every interaction, from vendor communications to ceremony scripts, reflects a commitment to inclusivity and representation.

One of the fundamental ways to foster inclusivity is by using gender-neutral language. Traditional wedding language often leans towards gendered norms, referring to brides and grooms in distinct terms. Recognizing and adopting gender-neutral terms, such as "partners" or "couples," allows for a more expansive and inclusive representation that resonates with the diverse experiences within the LGBTQ+ community, including those of trans men.

In the realm of vendor communications, clarity and openness are paramount. When engaging with wedding professionals, trans men and their partners may find it beneficial to communicate their preferred language, pronouns, and any specific considerations related to their identity. Transparent communication sets the foundation for a collaborative and respectful relationship, ensuring that the vendors understand and respect the unique needs of the couple.

Wedding ceremonies, with their rich tapestry of rituals and vows, provide an opportunity for intentional language that honors diverse identities. Crafting ceremony scripts that use inclusive language allows every participant, regardless of gender identity, to feel seen and valued. This extends beyond the mere words spoken—it's about creating a ceremonial space where the love and commitment shared by the couple transcend societal expectations and embrace the authenticity of their journey.

Representation matters, and this holds true in the visual aspects of wedding planning. From photography to videography, ensuring that images and footage authentically represent the diverse identities within the celebration is a crucial aspect of inclusivity. Trans men deserve to see themselves reflected in the visual narratives of love and commitment, and professionals who understand the nuances of LGBTQ+ experiences play a pivotal role in achieving this representation.

Inclusive language goes beyond terminology; it encompasses a mindset of respect and understanding. Wedding professionals who actively educate themselves on LGBTQ+ issues, including the experiences of trans individuals, contribute to creating an industry that is not only diverse but also welcoming. Couples, in turn, benefit from working with professionals who approach their celebration with an inclusive and affirming perspective.

Family and friends, as integral parts of the wedding journey, also play a role in ensuring inclusive language and representation. Encouraging open conversations about preferred pronouns, identities, and language choices fosters a supportive environment. By collectively embracing inclusive language, the support network becomes a powerful ally in affirming the experiences of trans men throughout the wedding planning process.

In conclusion, ensuring inclusive language and representation is a commitment to creating a wedding planning experience that honors the beautifully diverse spectrum of love. It's about acknowledging that every love story is unique, every identity is valid, and every celebration is an opportunity to embrace the richness of human connection. As we navigate this aspect of wedding planning, may our words and representations reflect the respect, understanding, and celebration that define the true essence of love in all its forms.

CHAPTER 11

Managing Stress and Wellness

In the whirlwind of wedding planning, amidst the joyous anticipation of a life-changing celebration, there exists another facet that deserves our attention—the well-being of the couples embarking on this incredible journey. Chapter 11 is a tender exploration of managing stress and prioritizing wellness, recognizing that the path to a wedding is not just about crafting a beautiful event but also about nurturing the emotional and physical well-being of those at the heart of the celebration.

Wedding planning, while exhilarating, can also be a source of stress as couples navigate a myriad of decisions, expectations, and timelines. This chapter invites you to take a pause, a collective breath, and reflect on the importance of prioritizing self-care and wellness throughout this transformative process. From the excitement of envisioning your dream ceremony to the intricacies of managing details, this chapter is a gentle reminder that your well-being is an essential part of the celebration.

We'll delve into strategies for managing stress, offering insights into effective communication, time management, and building a strong support system. Recognizing that every couple's journey is unique, we explore adaptable approaches that resonate with diverse personalities and lifestyles. Whether you're a couple planning an intimate elopement or a grand ceremony, the principles of stress management and wellness remain universal.

The chapter is not just about coping with stress; it's an exploration of cultivating joy, mindfulness, and resilience during a momentous chapter of your lives. We'll touch upon practices that foster emotional connection, mindfulness exercises that ground you in the present, and the importance of celebrating milestones along the way.

As you navigate the intricate dance of wedding planning, may this chapter serve as a guide to not only creating a beautiful celebration but also fostering a journey that is grounded in well-being. Your love story is a tapestry woven with threads of joy, connection, and commitment, and taking care of yourselves is an integral part of ensuring that the tapestry unfolds with grace and resilience.

Together, let's embark on this exploration of managing stress and prioritizing wellness—a journey that celebrates not just the destination but every step along the way. May your wedding planning be a testament to the beauty of love, care, and the enduring strength that comes from nurturing your well-being throughout this extraordinary adventure.

Prioritizing Self-Care During Wedding Planning

Amidst the excitement and busyness of wedding planning, it's easy for couples to find themselves caught up in a whirlwind of decisions, timelines, and expectations. In the midst of crafting the perfect celebration, it's crucial to carve out intentional moments for self-care, recognizing that the well-being of the individuals at the heart of the celebration is just as significant as the event itself.

One of the foundational pillars of self-care during wedding planning is effective communication. As a couple, establishing open and honest channels of communication lays the groundwork for mutual support. Share your thoughts, feelings, and concerns with your partner, creating a space where both voices are heard and validated. This collaborative approach not only strengthens your connection but also provides emotional support during moments of stress.

Time management becomes an invaluable tool in the arsenal of self-care. While wedding planning involves a myriad of tasks and timelines, it's essential to set realistic expectations and prioritize tasks based on their importance and deadlines. Avoid the temptation to tackle everything at once, and instead, break down the process into manageable steps. This approach allows for a more balanced distribution of energy and minimizes the likelihood of feeling overwhelmed.

Building a support system is another key element of prioritizing self-care. Surround yourself with friends, family, or even a wedding planning professional who understands the nuances of the process. Having a reliable support network provides a sounding board for ideas, a source of encouragement during challenging moments, and a reminder that you don't have to navigate this journey alone.

Mindfulness and intentional breaks are powerful tools in the realm of self-care. Incorporate moments of mindfulness into your routine, whether through meditation, deep breathing exercises, or simply taking a moment to savor the present. These intentional breaks serve as anchors, grounding you in the midst of a bustling planning process and fostering a sense of calm.

Celebrate milestones, both big and small, along the way. The journey to your wedding day is filled with achievements, from finalizing the guest list to choosing the perfect venue. Take the time to acknowledge and celebrate these accomplishments, recognizing the progress you've made. This practice not only instills a sense of achievement but also infuses joy into the planning process.

Physical well-being is intertwined with self-care, and maintaining a healthy lifestyle during wedding planning contributes to overall wellness. Prioritize adequate sleep, stay hydrated, and incorporate physical activity into your routine. A well-nourished and rested body enhances resilience, allowing you to approach challenges with clarity and vitality.

Ultimately, self-care is a personalized journey, and couples are encouraged to explore practices that resonate with their unique needs and preferences. Whether it's a quiet evening together, a shared hobby, or a pampering self-care ritual, the goal is to infuse moments of nourishment and rejuvenation into the wedding planning journey.

In essence, prioritizing self-care during wedding planning is an investment in the well-being of the couple and the resilience of their relationship. It's a commitment to nurturing not only the event itself but also the individuals at the heart of the celebration. As you navigate the intricate dance of planning, may self-care be a guiding principle, reminding you that the journey is as significant as the destination, and your well-being is an integral part of the love story you're crafting together.

Handling Family and Social Pressures

Wedding planning, while a celebration of love, often comes with its fair share of external expectations and societal pressures. Navigating family dynamics and social expectations can be a delicate dance, requiring couples to balance their own vision with the desires and opinions of those around them. In this section, we explore strategies for handling family and social pressures, ensuring that the planning process remains a journey centered on the couple's unique love story.

Open communication is the cornerstone of addressing family pressures. Honest conversations with both sets of parents, siblings, and other close relatives allow for an exchange of perspectives. Share your vision for the wedding and listen to their expectations. Finding common ground often involves compromise, and creating an environment where everyone feels heard fosters understanding and unity.

Establishing boundaries is a crucial aspect of handling family pressures. While it's natural for loved ones to be invested in the wedding planning process, couples must define their limits and communicate them clearly. Whether it's setting boundaries on the level of involvement or outlining specific decisions that are non-negotiable, creating a framework for respectful collaboration preserves the autonomy of the couple.

When faced with conflicting opinions, couples may find it helpful to designate a spokesperson. This can be a family member or friend who is skilled in diplomacy and can mediate discussions. Having a neutral party to convey the couple's decisions can mitigate potential conflicts and ensure that the planning process remains a positive and collaborative experience.

Couples should also prioritize their own needs and desires, remembering that the wedding is a reflection of their love story. It's natural to want to please family and friends, but the essence of the celebration should align with the couple's values and vision. Taking the time to articulate what aspects of the wedding are most meaningful to them allows couples to make decisions that resonate with their unique journey.

In some cases, seeking professional guidance, such as a wedding planner or counselor, can provide valuable support. Professionals experienced in managing family dynamics and social pressures can offer insights, mediate discussions, and help couples navigate complex situations. Their expertise can be particularly beneficial when cultural or religious expectations add layers of complexity to the planning process.

Flexibility is a key attribute in handling family pressures. As plans evolve, unforeseen challenges may arise. Couples are encouraged to approach these challenges with a mindset of adaptability. Whether it's adjusting certain aspects of the celebration or finding creative solutions that honor both familial expectations and the couple's vision, flexibility allows for a more harmonious planning process.

Lastly, remember that the love and commitment at the core of the celebration are what truly matter. While external pressures may arise, the foundation of the wedding is the unique bond shared by the couple. Embracing this truth allows couples to navigate family and social pressures with grace, keeping the focus on the joyous celebration of their love.

In conclusion, handling family and social pressures is an integral part of wedding planning. It's a delicate dance that requires communication, boundaries, and flexibility. By approaching these challenges with empathy and a commitment to honoring the couple's unique journey, the planning process can be a harmonious and joyous experience, paving the way for a celebration that reflects the authenticity of the love being celebrated.

Utilizing LGBTQ+ Support Networks

In the vibrant tapestry of wedding planning, couples within the LGBTQ+ community often find solace, understanding, and valuable resources within dedicated support networks. This section explores the importance of tapping into LGBTQ+ support networks during the wedding planning journey, offering a sense of community, shared experiences, and guidance that can be particularly affirming for couples navigating the intricacies of non-traditional celebrations.

One of the primary benefits of LGBTQ+ support networks is the opportunity for couples to connect with others who share similar experiences and perspectives. These networks serve as virtual or local communities where individuals can share stories, seek advice, and find inspiration. This sense of shared camaraderie fosters a feeling of belonging, assuring couples that they are not alone in their journey.

Navigating the nuances of LGBTQ+ weddings often involves addressing unique challenges and embracing non-traditional elements. LGBTQ+ support networks provide a wealth of knowledge and resources specific to the community's needs. Whether it's information on inclusive vendors, advice on handling potential roadblocks, or creative ideas that celebrate diverse identities, these networks empower couples with insights that resonate with their experiences.

Support networks also play a crucial role in providing emotional support. Wedding planning, while a joyful endeavor, can sometimes be accompanied by moments of stress or uncertainty. Having a community that understands the intricacies of LGBTQ+ celebrations allows couples to share their joys and challenges with individuals who genuinely comprehend the journey, offering empathy, encouragement, and a sense of solidarity.

Visibility and representation within LGBTQ+ support networks contribute to a broader narrative of inclusivity. Seeing diverse love stories celebrated within these communities reinforces the notion that every love story is valid and deserving of recognition. Couples can draw inspiration from a myriad of experiences, finding creative ideas that resonate with their unique identities and relationships.

Online platforms, social media groups, and LGBTQ+ events are avenues where couples can actively engage with these support networks. From forums discussing wedding planning tips to Instagram accounts showcasing diverse celebrations, the digital landscape provides a wealth of opportunities for connection. Attending LGBTQ+ events, whether virtual or in person, further strengthens these connections by fostering in-person interactions and networking.

Within these support networks, couples may find mentors or experienced individuals who have walked a similar path. These mentorships can be invaluable, providing guidance on navigating both the joys and challenges of wedding planning. Learning from the experiences of those who have already celebrated their love in a non-traditional way offers a wealth of insights and a sense of reassurance.

Inclusivity is a central theme within LGBTQ+ support networks. These communities often celebrate the intersections of diverse identities, recognizing that every couple's journey is unique. Couples can explore a myriad of perspectives, cultural influences, and creative expressions, contributing to the tapestry of LGBTQ+ love stories.

In essence, utilizing LGBTQ+ support networks during wedding planning is not only practical but also profoundly affirming. It's a way for couples to connect with a broader community that understands, supports, and celebrates the intricacies of their love story. As you navigate the journey of planning your wedding, may the connections you form within these networks serve as a source of strength, inspiration, and a reminder that love, in all its beautiful forms, is truly something to be celebrated.

Post-Wedding Reflection and Future Planning

As the echoes of your wedding day linger in the air and you embark on the journey beyond the ceremony, Chapter 12 invites you to step into the realm of post-wedding reflection and future planning. This chapter serves as a compass, guiding you through the terrain of reflection on your wedding experience and laying the groundwork for the exciting adventures that lie ahead as a married couple.

The period following your wedding is a unique juncture—a time to pause, breathe, and immerse yourselves in the memories of the celebration. Post-wedding reflection is not just about reminiscing; it's an opportunity to savor the joy, laughter, and love that filled your special day. Together, let's explore the significance of this reflective journey and the ways it can deepen your connection as partners.

While reflection is a beautiful aspect of the post-wedding period, future planning is equally vital. Your journey as a married couple is an unfolding story, and this chapter delves into the exciting prospects that await you. From setting shared goals to envisioning your life together, future planning is a collaborative venture that paves the way for a fulfilling and purposeful union.

The chapter is not merely a guide but a companion, offering insights and prompts to spark meaningful conversations between you and your partner. It encourages you to celebrate not only the culmination of your wedding planning efforts but also the beginning of a new chapter—one that is shaped by your shared dreams, aspirations, and a commitment to building a life filled with love and adventure.

As you turn the pages of this chapter, may it be a source of inspiration, reflection, and anticipation. Your wedding day is a milestone, and the journey that unfolds beyond it is a canvas waiting for the brushstrokes of your shared experiences. Together, let's navigate the terrain of post-wedding reflection and future planning, savoring the memories of the day you said "I do" and envisioning the countless "I dos" that await in the chapters yet to be written.

Reflecting on Your Wedding Experience

As the last strains of your wedding playlist fade away and the bouquet toss becomes a memory, the post-wedding period beckons with a unique sense of tranquility and nostalgia. Chapter 13 invites you to embark on the first step of this reflective journey—savoring and exploring the tapestry of your wedding experience.

Reflection is a poignant exercise that allows you and your partner to revisit the magical moments, the laughter shared, and the overwhelming love that enveloped your celebration. It's not just about reminiscing; it's about delving into the emotions, the unexpected surprises, and the tiny details that made your day uniquely yours.

Begin by revisiting your vows—the promises you made to each other in front of your loved ones. Reflect on the significance of those words and how they resonate with the journey you've embarked upon. Consider the readings, the music, and the symbolic gestures that wove a narrative around your love story. These elements, carefully chosen, are the threads that form the fabric of your wedding day.

Explore the photographs that captured fleeting moments—a stolen glance, a heartfelt embrace, or the joyous laughter that erupted spontaneously. Photographs are not merely images; they are portals that transport you back to the emotions, the ambiance, and the energy of that magical day. Take your time to immerse yourselves in these visual reminders of the love and celebration that surrounded you.

Consider the unique elements that made your wedding distinctly yours. Whether it was a personalized ceremony script, a meaningful ritual, or a specific choice in decor, reflect on how these elements reflected your personalities and love story. The quirks, the humor, and the personal touches are the brushstrokes that painted the canvas of your celebration.

Reflecting on your wedding experience is an opportunity to acknowledge the efforts of those who contributed to the day's success. From the vendors who brought your vision to life to the friends and family who stood by you, take a moment to express gratitude. Consider reaching out with heartfelt thank-you notes, sharing the impact they had on making your celebration truly special.

During this reflective journey, it's natural to encounter moments that were not as planned—perhaps a minor hiccup or a deviation from the script. Embrace these moments with grace, recognizing that they add character to your wedding story. The unplanned moments often become the anecdotes you'll fondly recount in the years to come.

As you navigate the reflections of your wedding experience, engage in open conversations with your partner. Share your favorite moments, the surprises that warmed your hearts, and the emotional highlights that left a lasting impression. Through these conversations, you not only deepen your connection but also gain insights into the nuances of each other's experience.

In essence, reflecting on your wedding experience is a gentle unraveling of the threads that wove together to create a day filled with love and joy. It's a tribute to the journey you've embarked upon as a married couple and a celebration of the love that surrounds and sustains you. As you immerse yourselves in this reflective journey, may the memories of your wedding day become cherished treasures that illuminate the path ahead.

Building a Strong Foundation for Your Marriage

Beyond the euphoria of the wedding day lies the terrain of marriage —an expansive landscape waiting to be explored and nurtured. Chapter 13 ventures into the realm of future planning, beginning with the essential task of building a strong foundation for your lifelong journey together.

Marriage is not merely a destination; it is an ongoing journey filled with shared experiences, challenges, and growth. As you step into this chapter of your life, consider it an opportunity to intentionally lay the groundwork for a resilient and fulfilling partnership.

Open communication is the cornerstone of a strong marital foundation. Reflect on the communication dynamics that unfolded during your wedding planning. Were there moments of seamless understanding? Did you navigate challenges with patience and empathy? Building on these experiences, strive to create a space where open and honest communication is not only encouraged but cherished.

Shared values and goals are the scaffolding upon which a strong marriage stands. Take the time to explore your individual aspirations and dreams, and discuss how they align with the collective vision for your life together. Whether it's career ambitions, family planning, or personal growth, a shared roadmap contributes to a sense of unity and purpose.

Embrace the lessons learned during the wedding planning process— lessons in compromise, collaboration, and navigating the unexpected. Apply these insights to your marriage, recognizing that flexibility and adaptability are invaluable traits in the face of life's twists and turns. The ability to weather storms together strengthens the foundation of your partnership.

Create rituals and traditions that are unique to your marriage. Whether it's a weekly date night, a special anniversary celebration, or a shared hobby, these rituals become the glue that binds you together. They serve as reminders of the intentional effort to nurture your connection amidst the busyness of life.

Financial planning is a practical aspect of building a strong foundation. Reflect on the budgeting and financial decisions made during your wedding planning, and extend this awareness to your shared financial future. Establishing a solid financial foundation involves open discussions about budgeting, savings, and long-term goals.

Consider the importance of individual growth within the context of partnership. Reflect on the ways in which you can support each other's personal aspirations and encourage individual development. A strong marriage is not about losing individual identities but rather about growing together while honoring each other's unique journeys.

Prioritize self-care within the marriage. Reflect on the moments during your wedding planning when stress levels peaked, and consider how you supported each other during those times. Apply this awareness to your ongoing journey, recognizing the importance of self-care practices that contribute to individual well-being and, by extension, the well-being of the marriage.

Celebrate the joyous moments that unfold within your marriage, both big and small. Reflect on the delight you experienced during your wedding day, and carry this spirit of celebration into your everyday lives. Whether it's a shared accomplishment, a spontaneous adventure, or a quiet moment of connection, find joy in the journey.

In conclusion, building a strong foundation for your marriage is a thoughtful and ongoing process. It involves reflection, intentional communication, and a shared commitment to nurturing the bond you've created. As you venture into the chapters ahead, may the foundation you lay become the bedrock of a resilient, joyful, and enduring partnership—a partnership that grows more vibrant with each passing day.

Navigating Life Beyond the Wedding Day

The wedding day, while a beautiful milestone, is just the beginning of a lifelong adventure that unfolds through the tapestry of marriage. Chapter 13 now turns its focus to the expansive terrain that awaits beyond the wedding day—a landscape filled with shared joys, challenges, and the rich tapestry of everyday life.

Life beyond the wedding day is a journey of continuous discovery. As partners, you'll find yourselves navigating through the ebb and flow of daily routines, career aspirations, family dynamics, and unforeseen challenges. Embracing the dynamic nature of life and maintaining a sense of curiosity about each other's evolving selves is key to fostering a thriving partnership.

Celebrate the small moments. While the wedding day is a grand celebration, the beauty of marriage lies in the ordinary, everyday moments. Whether it's sharing a quiet breakfast, conquering a household project together, or simply enjoying a lazy Sunday morning, find joy in the simplicity of shared moments. These seemingly mundane experiences contribute to the richness of your shared story.

Embrace change as a constant companion. Life is marked by seasons of change—career shifts, relocations, family expansions, and personal growth. Recognize that growth, both individually and as a couple, is a natural part of the journey. Adaptability and openness to change create a resilient partnership that can weather the shifting tides of life.

Prioritize quality time together. Amidst the hustle and bustle of life, intentional moments of connection become vital. Reflect on the significance of quality time during your wedding planning—moments when decisions were made together, dreams were shared, and laughter echoed through the process. Carry this spirit of togetherness into your everyday lives.

Support each other's individual pursuits. As you navigate life together, honor the unique aspirations and passions that shape each of you. Reflect on the encouragement and support you provided during the wedding planning, and extend this support to individual endeavors. A thriving partnership is one that fosters the growth and fulfillment of each partner.

Cultivate a sense of gratitude. Reflect on the moments of gratitude you experienced during your wedding day—the love of family and friends, the support of loved ones, and the joy of being surrounded by those who cherish your union. Carry this spirit of gratitude into your marriage, expressing appreciation for the everyday gestures, shared experiences, and the love that continues to flourish.

Navigate challenges as a team. Challenges are inevitable, and life beyond the wedding day may present hurdles that demand resilience and unity. Reflect on the moments during your wedding planning when challenges were overcome through collaboration and mutual support. These experiences serve as a foundation for facing future challenges as a united front.

Continuously communicate and reassess. Reflect on the effectiveness of communication during your wedding planning—how it facilitated decisions, resolved conflicts, and strengthened your connection. Communication remains a cornerstone of a thriving marriage. Regularly check in with each other, reassess your shared goals, and ensure that your individual aspirations align with the evolving narrative of your partnership.

Celebrate milestones and create new traditions. Reflect on the joyous milestones of your wedding day and consider how these celebrations enriched your connection. As you journey through marriage, continue to mark significant moments—anniversaries, achievements, and shared milestones. Create new traditions that hold personal meaning, contributing to the legacy of your shared journey.

In essence, navigating life beyond the wedding day is a continuous exploration of love, growth, and shared experiences. It involves embracing the beauty in the ordinary, adapting to change, and nurturing the dynamic evolution of your partnership. As you traverse this expansive terrain, may your marriage be a tapestry woven with threads of joy, resilience, and the enduring love that started on the day you said "I do."